Contents

1 The enterprise of living

Life is a journey, but how often do people think of that journey as anything more than a series of steps through time? We are born, we grow up, we work and marry and bring up children, we grow old and we die. The peak of the journey is reached at some unspecified time in early adult life, and thereafter it is a long decline.

For some people, that is perhaps all that there is to it—'birth, and copulation, and death', as T. S. Eliot says in Sweeney Agonistes. *But it is our belief, and our experience, that human beings can grow and develop throughout their lives, that to travel hopefully and with enjoyment on that long journey is a real possibility for most of us, that every stage has its own challenges and its own fascination.*

We believe that our experience of, and response to, the challenges of each stage can develop in us new qualities which enable us to face the challenges of the next and to reach the end of our days with a feeling of 'wholeness', what Shakespeare meant when he said 'Ripeness is all.'

The grit in the oyster

No one's life can be free of suffering and setbacks, and few people follow the orderly progression beloved of some theorists and popularly idealised as the 'fairy-tale existence'. As a matter of fact fairy tales and myths are not like that (think of the Babes in the Wood, or the Snow Queen, or Oedipus and the House of Atrius). Many such myths help us understand *real* life, in which uprooting, divorce, disability, disaster, disappointment and bereavement happen, even if not all to the same person at one time. These, as much as the joys and satisfactions, are the stuff of which new growth is made, the grit in the oyster that may eventually lead in the face of all odds to a serene and happy old age. The philosopher George Santayana once said, 'There is no cure for birth and death save to enjoy the interval.' We believe that nearly everyone can find a way to enjoy that interval, whether they have a natural talent for enjoyment or not; and that the way lies in developing the capacity for growth.

Nancy Kappler Foster

THE LIFE CYCLE SERIES

Growing Through Life

Rhona Rapoport
and
Robert Rapoport

HARPER & ROW, PUBLISHERS
New York Hagerstown Philadelphia
San Francisco London Sydney

This book was devised and produced
by Multimedia Publications Inc

General Editor: *Dr. Leonard Kristal*
Prod Mgr/Art Dir/Design: *Bob Vari*
Picture Researcher: *Judy Kristal*

First published in Holland 1980 by
Multimedia Publications Inc

British Library Cataloguing in Publication Data
Rapoport, Rhona
Rapoport, Robert

Growing Through Life

References pg. 122–124
Includes index

ISBN 06 384751 5 paper

Colour origination: United Artists Ltd, Israel
Typeset by CCC and printed in Great Britain by
William Clowes (Beccles) Limited, Beccles and London, England

Joy in life: the challenge is to turn bad times as well as good into chances to grow.

What this book will tell you

This book is about the way we grow and in growing find satisfactions in the enterprise of living, all through our lives. To this end we divide the life cycle into a series of *stages*, each of which is the subject of a separate chapter. Every stage is characterised by certain typical inner *preoccupations*, which are rooted in biology, and by outer *challenges* from the individual's environment.

The kind of psychological growth we shall be talking about takes place when the individual finds *opportunities* in the outside world that will channel and satisfy his or her preoccupations. This life task requires what we define as *resourcefulness*—resourcefulness in recognising one's inner preoccupations, and resourcefulness in responding to challenges as opportunities (whether provided by family, school, neighbourhood, friends, jobs, local facilities and amenities or anything else).

We believe that opportunities will be most effectively used as resources by individuals who have learned to develop *interests*, that the key to growth is the development of interests, and that interests form the essential link between our inner preoccupations and outer challenges. This capacity also helps individuals to make links between one stage of the life cycle and the next. Individuals vary greatly in their resourcefulness, and social environments vary greatly in the opportunities they offer. We shall argue that society should provide opportunities and at the same time encourage individual resourcefulness.

Growth has many meanings

The concept of growth has been used in psychology and the social sciences in various ways. When applied to *personal* development it has, on the whole, been linked to *biological* growth, with its emphasis on growing up to maturity, to be followed inevitably by decline and death. Biological growth is relatively easy to measure—height, weight, muscle development, neurological responses, eyesight, hearing, speed, strength, stamina and so on. Its message is that the human organism matures to a peak in early adult life and then declines along predictable lines.

G. Stanley Hall, sometimes reckoned to be the founder of developmental psychology, based his concept of personal growth on the Darwinian theories of evolution. 'Ontogeny recapitulates phylogeny,' he wrote at the turn of the century.[1] He meant that the developing individual goes through stages from primitive to advanced, much as did the orders and species of the animal world in the course of evolution.

Because of this, developmental psychology as a scientific study has tended to be confined to the age groups up to, and sometimes including, adolescence, at which point full biological maturity is reached: this is the point to which we, as a species, have evolved.

The very term 'developmental psychology' is often used interchangeably with 'child psychology'. The development of *intelligence*, particularly in children, has been closely studied and constitutes a very sophisticated field of scientific research and knowledge (see, for example, the works of the Swiss psychologist Jean Piaget). The development of *language* and *thought* in the child is also well charted, from simple symbolic operations to the capacity for hypothetico-deductive, or logical, reasoning at the age of eleven or twelve.

The development of children's *behaviour patterns* has also received a lot of attention (beginning with the work of Arnold Gesell at Yale and Charlotte Buhler in Vienna, amplified by later studies at the University of California at Berkeley, and at the Fels Institute in Detroit). And ever since Freud, psychoanalysts have studied the inner drives and emotional complexes which characterise and complicate the dynamics of development. They have emphasised the importance of the child's *emotional* development and of its early life experience in forming its character and thereby moulding later responses to life. Finally, the school of psychology associated with the name of Kurt Lewin (the 'field' or *Gestalt* psychologists) has emphasised the importance of the childhood environment in determining patterns of development (for a résumé of the work of developmental psychologists, see *Understanding Psychology* in the Life Cycle Series).

How does growth occur?

The ways in which growth occurs have been explained in terms of three classical sets of factors: biological maturation; environmental influences and experiences; and social transmission (education). The theory you subscribe to determines how much importance you assign to each of these. More recently, Piaget and his colleagues have proposed a fourth factor, called 'progressive equilibration'.[2] By this they mean that there is an inner force, something in a person that is not biological but emerges at each stage as a product of the elements of his or her development. It brings about, with varying degrees of intentional effort, a new balance.

Much of the work in developmental psychology is devoted to refining and extending these formulations. There have been a number of integrative approaches to the study of development in the work of people such as Paul Mussen, John Conger and Jerome Kagan.

A lifelong process

This is more important than it may at first sound: it is only recently that psychoanalysts, who previously assumed that all significant development of personality occurred in the first few years of life, have come to acknowledge that development may be possible *throughout* life. Though Jung was interested in this possibility, emphasising the more spiritual elements of personality development, he was not widely influential in his own lifetime. Erik Erikson and other psychoanalytically oriented psychologists have taken up this theme, and it is now being worked on rather more widely.[3]

A crisis can be positive

Taking the whole life cycle as our frame, a number of concepts are useful. The concept of *crisis* or turning point is used, not only in the sense of unexpected or traumatic event, but to denote the ordinary, expectable critical transitions that punctuate life—birth, school entry, marriage, having children, changes of job, bereavement.[4] We have used an adaptation of the developmental approach applied to whole families by Reuben Hill and his associates.[5] Also useful has been the work of Gerald Caplan, particularly his analysis of families and other social relationships as 'support systems' for individuals trying to cope with life's challenges.[6]

Life is never static: but even traumatic disruptions can be part of our growth.

We approach the study of growth throughout life by viewing ordinary lives as sequences of stages, each associated with characteristic inner preoccupations. Growth occurs when there is an adaptive transition from one stage to the next as life's critical events present themselves. Each transition is accomplished by dealing with the specific tasks or challenges associated with that transition.

To explain the mechanisms by which individuals cope with the tasks of transition, we have three additional concepts, as noted above: *interest* on the individual's side, *opportunity* on the side of the social environment, *resourcefulness* as the quality which allows for the translation of interests into action, using available opportunities.

We are concerned with how people put together a 'whole life' out of the events and experiences that come their way.[7]

Life-enhancing interests

The concept of personal interests was first developed in the social sciences for vocational guidance. If people find themselves in occupations which do not really match their personal interests, boredom and poor job performance are likely to result. The failure to fit interests to occupations is obviously undesirable, so batteries of tests were designed to identify a person's interests and to guide him into a suitable occupation. The Kuder Preference Record and the Strong Vocational Interest Blank (SVIB) are two such tests.

These are not intelligence or IQ tests: interests are different from and not directly correlated with intelligence. For example, accountants and artists will generally have contrasting interests, though both groups are likely to rank high on intelligence.

A variety of studies show that interests are discernible by puberty; and they tend to persist, especially if a 'correct' choice of occupation is made. Specific occupations tend to require a certain uniformity of interests in their followers, and these do not change much, or at least not quickly: bankers now are

Chances are, if they enjoy competing at this age, they'll be better equipped later

interested in much the same things as bankers in 1930, in spite of the radical changes that banking has undergone since then.[8]

Bridging the inner and outer worlds

Our own concern is not with this kind of vocational matching, which has been comprehensively dealt with by others, but with the larger concept of 'whole life interests', interests relating to family and leisure as well as to occupation. These are bridges between a person's inner drives and the opportunities and constraints in his or her social environment.

The set of underlying personal preoccupations characteristic of each stage can be expressed through different interests—family life, work, cultural ideas. Channelling these interests means entering into different sorts of activities. Expressing interests tends to link people to other people. Though some interests are expressed in solitary activity, like fishing or playing solitaire, they are learned in the culture and therefore in a sense always shared.

Chances of a lifetime

The resourceful use of opportunities to express interests stimulates growth, permits continued involvement in life, and brings satisfaction. We decline in our physical powers as we grow older, but there is no reason to think that we decline similarly in our capacity to develop or express interests. Whether we continue to develop this capacity is affected by past experiences as well as by innate differences between one person and another. These experiences are affected, in turn, by the nature of outside opportunities. But the opportunities themselves do not determine growth: they must be used by individuals for this purpose.

By developing interests, we can tap our endless capacity to explore new areas within ourselves.

All this may sound blandly optimistic in the light of the evidence around us of the plight of people apparently unable to

develop satisfying life interests. The 'captive housewife' with many cares and few supports who later becomes the 'empty nest' mother with time on her hands but few skills or interests and perhaps little sexual attractiveness are the subjects of much contemporary lament. So too are the harried middle-aged 'workaholic' with an ulcer in his gut and a coronary on the way, the divorcee facing life as a single parent, who feels guilty, inadequate, poor and socially isolated, and the retired worker deprived of his job, his main psychological prop, who lacks both education and experience because his work began so early and was all he ever knew.

Nevertheless, we believe that continuous growth is possible throughout life; that it does in fact occur; and that we can learn how to grow through life by examining the interaction of interest, resourcefulness and opportunity in people's lives as they move from stage to stage of the life cycle.

The life cycle

All ways of dividing up our lives are more or less arbitrary. Shakespeare did it one way, with his seven ages of man. Biologists have their own ground plan—infancy, puberty, prime of life, senility. Sociologists do it by stages linked to the cycle of social institutions such as school, family and occupation, marriage, parenthood, then retirement. In her lively book *Passages*, the writer Gail Sheehy divides life into decades—Pulling Up Roots (the teens), the Trying Twenties, Catch-30, the Deadline Decade.[9]

In this book we define the stages of life slightly differently. Using a combination of psychological and sociological criteria, we use five stages: childhood, adolescence, young adulthood, the establishment phase, and the later years. Our categories are also arbitrary. Variations in people's life patterns blur the boundary lines. But this fits modern life. People or their families are not 'in the wrong' simply because they do not fit a pattern in every detail. A man who is in his later years and married to a much younger woman need not feel nowadays that he is 'abnormal'; nor need a woman married to a younger man. It would be wrong to pretend that departing from the 'norm' or timetable associated with the principal life events does not raise special challenges, but these are rarely insuperable. It is not necessary to worry excessively about being out of step, because people's rate of maturing and their circumstances in life vary enormously. And in our society, we value diversity as the spice of life.

The five stages of life

The five stages that we present cover the whole cycle of a human life. We think they are valid for all cultures, not just our own.

Childhood embraces several substages, from earliest infancy to school entry and primary education.

Adolescence is taken to be roughly between the ages of 13 and 19. The main preoccupation in this phase is with the search for 'identity', to find out who one is as a distinct individual, not just as a pale reflection of one's parents.

Young adulthood starts at the time of leaving school, when one is catapulted into a more adult role or goes to university or college. Here people are preoccupied with learning to commit themselves to intimate relationships and social institutions such as marriage and work. This stage lasts until they have 'settled down', probably with the first child (though not all will want children or marriage) and are becoming established as full adults.

The establishment phase occurs, very approximately, between the ages of 25 and 55. The main preoccupations here are with making the kind of commitments that will constitute satisfying life investments—in work, family, friends and leisure activities. Commitments may also be to abstract notions such as political or religious ideologies. In this stage, more than 90 per cent of adults are married; and most have children. By the end of the stage the children will mostly be launched on their own journey through life.

Later years are marked by a preoccupation with attaining a sense of social and personal integration, and the acceptance of mortality.

Through all life's many changes, some simple pleasures remain the same.

The triple helix

In all these stages we see an interaction of three aspects of life—leisure, work and family. Each aspect has its own sequence of stages and forms a kind of 'career'. We think of the careers as forming a spiral, or helix, rather than a straight line or steps, because when a person enters each new phase adjustment to it is achieved partly by going back over earlier experiences. Thus, when a young woman becomes a mother and nurses her baby she relives, in a sense, her own infantile relationship with her mother. This contributes both to the way she mothers her own child and to the way she revises her current relationship with her mother. It may also affect her leisure activities and her employment career. Together the three interlocking careers form what we have called 'the triple helix', each with a logic and life course of its own, each affecting the others.

Nowadays most people would reckon that in practical terms there is a fairly clear distinction between these three aspects of life. 'Work' is paid employment, normally occupies about eight hours of the day away from the home and family, and by some definitions is the *opposite* of leisure. 'Family' is a set of intimate relationships, partly duty, partly a haven, and ideally a source of pride and pleasure. 'Leisure' is usually defined as the time left over from these two involvements, though for many people leisure, defined as enjoyment, is fused to some extent with one or both of the other two. In leisure, one can develop personal interests, whether in sport or nature, books or photography. But personal interests can also be pursued at work or in family life.

Leisure and interests

Leisure seems in recent times to have become a rather self-conscious category. In traditional societies, prior to industrialisation, work, play and family meshed together more closely in the daily life of most people: craftsmen like cobblers, bakers and blacksmiths lived 'over the shop', with family life, children's

Working hard at leisure: these days, big business.

play and work all intermingled; the farmer's wife milked the cows, and the children fed the chickens and geese, and together everyone above the age of four brought in the harvest and prepared for and enjoyed harvest festival, as well as the 150 other high days and holidays of the pre-industrial year. There is still an echo of that world in the corner shop or public house or hotel where husband, wife and family are the workforce. In the early industrial age, many children went with their parents to the factories, or took their turn at the looms in weavers' cottages, and there was little time for 'leisure', so exhausting was the rest of life.

Intertwining strands

We are not suggesting that the past was a golden age and that today our lives are totally disintegrated. Even in our fragmented modern world, the three strands of leisure, work and family are more intertwined than people may suspect. One of the dynamic forces that makes each of the strands develop into a spiral, or helix, is the development of *interests*. Interests are something we get involved with. They are not confined to our 'time off'; they may develop in and spill over from our work. Alternatively, they may develop in the home and be applied in the other spheres. The strands of life interlock.

So while leisure is a major potential breeding ground for interests, it is not the only one. It is the dominant strand at the beginning and the end of life (pre-school and retirement). In the prime of life, leisure is perceived by many people as being on the sidelines, a sort of reward for work, enjoyed at weekends and on holidays. Unemployment during one's middle years is a form of involuntary leisure—usually regarded as undesirable and sometimes disastrous for family life both economically and psychologically.

Interests, as we have observed, can be expressed in any of these fields; indeed they constitute the connective tissue linking one stage to the next. Regardless of where they are developed, interests can find expression in any part of one's life—work, family, leisure. We are concerned with how interests are channelled for the growth of the whole person rather than for any specific purpose such as vocational placement.

When interests mean trouble . . .

A lifestyle which allows no scope to express one's interests, whether in work, family or leisure, will produce malaise; the pattern of living must be changed or suffering will build up. A black youth in any large American or European city, preoccupied with identity in a mixed society and searching for stimulation—perhaps testing the tolerance of the white authorities—may roam the streets looking for 'something' which will provide an opportunity to channel his developing interest in excitement and new experiences. Unless he finds it through legally acceptable channels (and there are few of these), trouble with the law may become a focal point in his life. Interests can evolve on street corners, but unless there are opportunities to channel them constructively, they may be frustrated or become troublesome.

Our society favours youth in theory, the general assumption being that it has growth potential and is therefore worth taking trouble over. It therefore seems particularly tragic when young people are blocked or frustrated in the development of their interests through our failure to understand their specific preoccupations and to provide opportunities to develop interests based on them.

... and stability spells stagnation

Those who make it through to a stable lifestyle in middle age often confront another set of issues. Their preoccupation is with productivity, and later with the payoffs they expect from the life investments they have made. The danger, during the long 'plateau' of established family and career life, is of feeling stale, in a rut—or, if comfortable, bored. At worst, there is the risk of becoming psychologically depressed. This may be severe if the person becomes unemployed or finds it impossible to develop new interests and activities. A common source of difficulties is the assumption by employers and others that the middle aged are set in their ways and have little growth potential.

We argue here that people *do* have growth potential in middle age, but that the growth may relate to other areas of life than economic productivity. When there is frustration in job or career development, personal growth depends on alternative interests which can be channelled into other activities. It takes particularly great resourcefulness to develop these interests and discover and seize relevant opportunities at this stage of life, to add a second string to one's bow or develop a second career, but it *can* be done.

Getting oneself together

Resourcefulness is the capacity to bring about a fruitful interaction between outside forces and those inside oneself. Outside resources are partly provided by public authorities, partly by private enterprise; but many people's needs are not met by anyone, and some go completely unrecognised. To make use of outside resources, one needs to mobilise oneself. The old-fashioned Victorian value of self-help has been at risk of being thrown out with the bathwater of puritanism. There is much in the idea of self-help that is applicable today—some might say, more than ever. Mutual aid, another old-fashioned virtue, is being revived as a necessity in today's fragmented and impersonal world. Both values depend on our cultivating our own capacities and joining them voluntarily with the efforts of others to mutual advantage. Of all things in life, growth is something that cannot be done *for* you. Like a plant in a hothouse, growth can be helped, even forced, by environment, but not created. Unlike a plant, you yourself can help to create the conditions that facilitate your own growth.

'Hey I think I've discovered gravity!'—for children, every activity is part of the learning process.

2 Childhood: a time for play

Our conceptions of childhood have varied through the ages and in different societies. The French historian Philippe Ariès has documented for us how arbitrary the precise dividing lines are between childhood and adulthood, and indeed how recent in our culture is the whole idea of a separate stage of childhood. In 17th century Europe, for example, children were treated very much like adults, going through the same daily round of activities and participating in the same leisure pursuits.[1]

Sometimes, as in some pre-industrial societies, children have been thought of as not very valuable except for the work they could do, and parents have shown little personal involvement with them given the high infant mortality rates. More recently, children have been valued very highly indeed, anyway in the Western world. Parents have often been heard to say that no sacrifice was too great for them, though children no longer work for the family in the same way. A child is now valued for itself, and parents are now very absorbed in its healthy growth and development. Child-rearing and educational philosophies have veered from one extreme, emphasising the need to tame the aggressive, destructive aspects of the child's nature (those 'wicked' aspects dwelt on by the Puritans and their successors) to the other extreme, which stresses the child's essential goodness and potential for self-discovery. The first emphasis is seen in discipline-oriented education in the tradition of Dr Arnold, former headmaster of Rugby School, and in literature in William Golding's *Lord of the Flies*. The second is to be found in the Utopian writings of Jean-Jacques Rousseau and in the philosophies of Pestalozzi, the Swiss educator, and A. S. Neill, whose school at Summerhill advanced the progressive education movement in Britain.

Focus on mastery

Recently there has been recognition not only of the variety of conflicting theories of human nature, but of the complexity of the whole developmental process. The process *is* complex, to be sure, but certain outlines can be discerned. From the child's side,

'I know what it does—but how do you make it do it?'

the dominating tasks of this crucial stage of life centre on mastery—mastery of body functions, of language to communicate with others, of the ability to make one's way in the world—what psychologist Robert W. White has called 'a sense of interpersonal competence'. The key is growth towards autonomy by degrees, away from total dependence on the parents.

The child is motivated by two forces in the growth process—the drive towards autonomy on the one hand, and love for and attachment to the parents who have nurtured it on the other. The drive towards autonomy comes partly from within, partly (and this is heightened in adolescence) as a reaction against being controlled.

Playing is exploring

Childhood spans infancy, early childhood and schooldays and involves a number of different people and experiences. We shall give particular emphasis to the role of *play* in the growth process. Play is at the heart of the child's exploration of the world. Play makes learning more acceptable, and it offers the child a chance for experiment and the parent a chance for sharing the child's experience as opposed to merely imposing it.

But obviously play alone is not enough. Growth of the capacity to master the tasks of living requires disciplined learning.

School entry: start of a new life

School entry is a key growth point. New people come into the child's life. New methods of dealing with the world are observed and tried out. New caretakers become important. Parents, too, may be freed at this point for further growth as individuals, branching out in the development of their own interests as well as sharing time with the child.

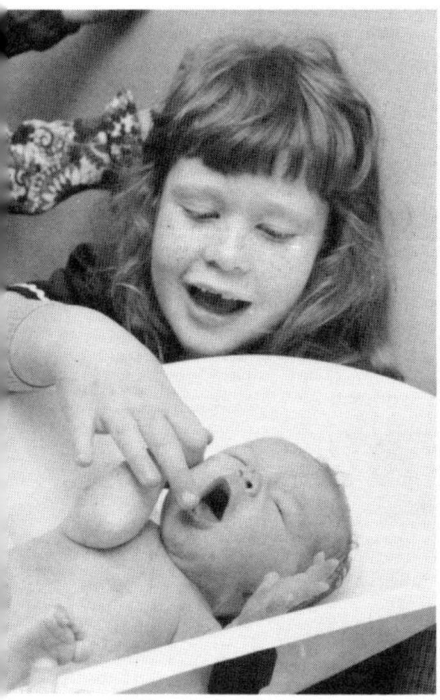

An ever-expanding circle of new people and new influences.

School entry is not usually a sudden plunge, though it may be. It is generally a gradual transition. The child may go to a nursery school before entering formal schooling. And even then there is usually a year or two, or even three, of infant teaching which allows a more play-like approach to learning before academic teaching methods are introduced. Whatever its particular approach, school offers the child a new, ever-widening world in which the seeds of interests sown in the family can be nurtured and new ones implanted. The child's world expands to include new places, new people, new things, new experiences, and in this expansion lies potential for growth. Play—in street games, playground games, picture games, pencil and paper games, songs, music and drama—helps make this potential an actuality.

Preoccupations of childhood

The child's preoccupations change as the world widens. Having come through the earlier preoccupations with body functions (the oral, anal and genital stages of psychic development which Freud studied so microscopically), the child has formed a core of personality which will serve, for better or worse, as a foundation for subsequent development. For a time, the mastery of instinctual drives shifts into the background and the child takes on intellectual challenges. This period, termed the 'latency

As the photograph is 'latent' on the undeveloped film, so the child's potential gradually takes shape.

period' by Freudians, lasts from the age of about six till puberty, when a new physical spurt brings the turbulence of adolescence.

There are different ways of viewing childhood experiences. They may be regarded as rooted in biology. Psychologists with an interest in education generally consider the child's preoccupations in these early school years reflect natural stages of cognitive, or intellectual, development. The theories of Jean Piaget, the Swiss psychologist, and of Arnold Gesell at Yale are influential examples of this approach, in which the child's growing capacity to perform such intellectual tasks as reasoning logically, or visualising geometrical forms, are charted in detail as the unfolding of a biologically based process, much as one would study the growth of a flower from seed.

Other psychologists have been concerned primarily with how the child *learns.* Learning theorists following the lead of the early behaviourist Watson have studied how responses to particular stimuli in the social environment become part of the child's store of habits, skills and information. Still others, the 'field theorists' in the tradition of Kurt Lewin, have studied developmental processes in an altogether broader context—the whole field of social forces, as opposed to specific stimuli.

The growth of interests

From our point of view, childhood experiences are crucial not only in the accumulation of a store of skills and information, but in the development of resourcefulness and the formation of interests. In this period a certain attitude or 'set' towards life's experiences develops which affects subsequent experiences. This does not mean that the die is cast in these early years and that if things aren't right there is no chance to alter them ever again, except in very extreme cases where children are severely deprived or maltreated. But the experiences of this phase are highly formative. The development of a consciousness that one can involve oneself meaningfully in life experiences, that interest can be found in them, is vital. A passion for *something* lays the groundwork. Childhood passions may wane or change, but if the capacity to develop enthusiastic involvements is stunted by fears or inhibitions, it may be hard to awaken later.

Resourcefulness in the development of interests has to be seen, of course, in a generic sense. It is not the specific interests that are crucial but the capacity to *be interested.* If a child is fascinated with painting, telling stories, reading, playing a penny whistle or football, it does not mean that these will be the specific activities that will serve him or her throughout life.

Assets for life

The particular activity through which an interest is expressed can change. Interests can be redeployed time and again in different activities later in life: an interest in music, say, can be expressed by playing a penny whistle at home or a trombone in the school band, attending concerts in adult life, listening to the radio or records in old age. An early interest in sport can be transferred from playing rough, competitive games to less physically taxing activities like swimming or cycling later in life. The crucial point is to use early opportunities to develop interests of some kind, to find stimulation in them and derive pleasure.

Why play is important

Sign him up, quick!

Play has an important role in the development of interests, which is why we concentrate here on play in the early formative years, rather than on relationships or formal learning. By now we are familiar, thanks to the work of developmental psychologists, with the idea that 'child's play' is not merely a diversionary or recreational activity, but a good part of the stuff of their life and quest for competence. When we say to one another 'What are you playing at?', or about another person 'He's just playing games with you', it is often with some irritation, and far from fun. Children, however, need to play, and play is instrumental for their mental and emotional growth.[2] (Adults also need play, not only for recreation but as an important ingredient of a satisfactory lifestyle. Huizinga, the Dutch social historian, argues in his book *Homo Ludens* that serious formal education and work suppress people's innate capacity for playfulness, stifling creativity which could benefit society as a whole.)[3]

Charting and measuring children's growth through play is a different kind of task from charting and measuring their physical growth, or the increase in IQ scores or technical skills. Play lends itself less directly to quantification. Nevertheless, it has been carefully studied and described. Jean Piaget, Jerome Bruner and other developmental psychologists have provided a wealth of detail on the subject. Eurfron Gwynne-Jones has this to say on the different kinds of play and their functions at different ages:

> '. . . consider the activities of Kay, Lucian and Tristan, who have taken over the kitchen floor. They have a central pool of paints and are each attacking their paintings in their own way. Kay is two—she smells the paint, sloshes it around, tips some, then rubs it into the paper. Lucian, at three and a half, dips the paint brush into the pot and concentrates hard on his picture—a mass of blue strokes. Tristan, at five, is creating a whole world of fantasy and imagination on his paper—he has recognisable houses and people. If asked what they were doing, I suppose he would say, "*just playing* in the kitchen".'[4]

Laying the foundations

Between the ages of three and five, the foundations are laid for much of the child's 'set' towards experience, and therefore his capacity to grow. The sense of fun, excitement and pleasure that comes with new learning is as important as the skills themselves, for it is this positive feeling which attaches itself to new challenges as they arise, and allows the individual to tackle them self-confidently and resourcefully. Failing that, the child may regress into despair and passivity.

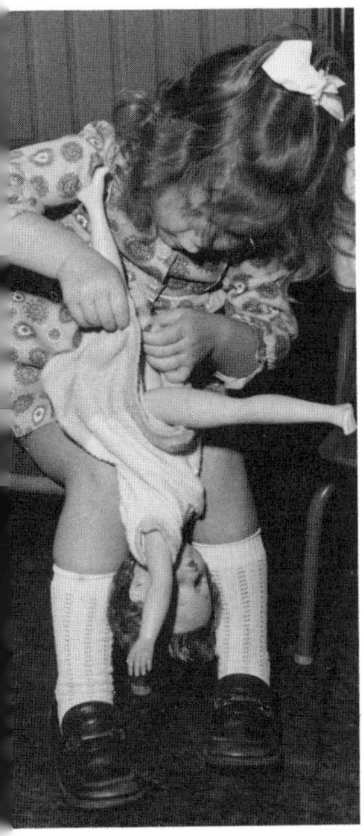

Through play we begin to learn who we are and what we can do.

The infant plays first with its own body, and with objects in its immediate environment, learning to distinguish the two. Toddlers playing together in the same room play with toys, but separately. This is called 'parallel play'. They have not yet learned to play co-operatively, but for each child the play provides opportunities to explore the world around. Through play children assimilate experiences into an intelligible pattern, and relate their own bodies and manipulative skills to objects.

Art is great fun for children and allows them to express a freshness and originality, a direct appeal to the senses that many adult painters, like Klee and Miró, have imitated. Through art the child is learning a skill—learning to observe, learning to co-ordinate his muscles as well as exercising his imagination and entering into a new kind of relationship with the world around him. The child may not initially distinguish between what is a suitable surface on which to play with paints and what is not, but this is a matter for parental guidance. It is up to adults to provide plenty of paper or other appropriate material instead of blaming the child for choosing walls or floors.

Sex differences

Through some indecipherable combination of innate differences and cultural influences young boys and young girls tend to favour different kinds of play. Boys generally prefer more physical pursuits—running, pushing, pulling, and rough and tumble. They tend more often to choose construction and building toys. Girls tend to prefer and are better at games involving words, dressing up and 'pretend' play, and non-aggressive social play. This does not, of course, mean that there aren't verbal, gentle boys, or aggressive, rough-and-tumble girls—there are. In many families and subcultures adults deliberately encourage similar play in children of both sexes—giving boys dolls to dress up, or construction toys to girls.

Triggers of playfulness

Some children are naturally more playful than others, but there are differences in the environment and in the approach to play that can bring out playfulness in children. It is important to be aware of these triggers and how they can be stimulated.

Family culture is an important factor. In some families there is a sense of playfulness and fun—whether innate or cultivated. The family may play with words, tell jokes, stimulate the child with amusing experiences. Basil Bernstein and other sociolinguists have studied how linguistic codes, as they call them, are more 'elaborated' in some (usually more educated and affluent) families than in others.[5] The stimulated child, who is talked to and taught an elaborated code of language, is one who will approach new situations with an exploratory, searching and testing attitude—an attitude which will be expressed in later stages through experimentation and reasoning.

Resources may be plentiful or scarce in the family culture and its associated social groups. There may be cars for trips to the country and visits to places of interest; radio, television and music for stimulating the senses; playpens and toys, books and pictures. Nowadays, there are also many toys which are specifically designed to be educational, so that the child learns by playing and finds out that learning can be fun.

It is obviously wrong if too much is made of material things. A child showered with expensive, elaborate toys may actually be prevented from learning to exercise ingenuity and imagination. Many affluent families push things on to the child in such a way as to spoil its fun, however unintentionally. Parents should watch themselves and trim presents and equipment to the needs of the child, and its readiness to use them enjoyably.

Playmates are obviously necessary to children, yet many parents do not know how to relate to playmates in a way their children will appreciate. Some may be fearful of undesirable influences, or envious of their children's delight at being so involved with others. They may cut off some of the exposure to others that could benefit their children's development. A good deal of both the learning and the enjoyment emerges from *social* aspects of play—learning to play co-operatively among differents sorts of children, according to rules, and taking into account that there are others involved who have ideas and feelings that may be different from one's own. Iona and Peter Opie have accumulated numerous instances of street and playground games that are passed along from generation to generation of children, half forgotten by adults (and therefore not usually taught by them), but clearly relevant in widening the child's horizons and helping

In playing with other children, the child learns that he is not only an individual—but also part of a society.

it deal with various feelings about getting along with others in the kind of world we live in.[6]

The wider culture may also be a trigger for the quality of infant experience. If children are expected to enjoy themselves, they have a different experience of early life than if they are expected to sit quietly, and if having fun is considered wicked—as in our puritanical past. In puritanical cultures there is less play, less enjoyment, and instead a sense that merit in life comes from hard work, endurance and suppression of 'selfish' or 'wicked' impulses. If, on the other hand, the culture encourages expressiveness, provides a rich lore of jokes and games, and opportunities for fun—whether zoos and museums or the seashore and farmyards—the child has a greater chance of enjoying the broadening experiences that play brings, and therefore learning to enjoy the idea of growing into new situations.

Attempts to characterise our whole society in any simple way are bound to be wrong because of the complexity and rapid change we are experiencing. However, it is probably true to say that we are a child-oriented society. We want our children to be happy; we wish to safeguard the rights of children—witness, for example, the manifesto of the United Nations' International Year of the Child. We try, as individuals and as families, to find time to play, to create (and press the relevant authorities to provide) facilities and resources for play, and to stimulate the sense of fun and playfulness that children, adults and society *all* need in their different ways. Yet, as a society, we are at odds with one another, often confused, and ineffective in finding ways and means to achieve these goals. We have to acknowledge that it is often an uphill struggle, despite the obvious value of encouraging joy in childhood.

Parents as facilitators

An awareness of how formative childhood experience is has increased parents' concern about what constitutes good parenting. It is no longer possible to be a good parent simply by imitating one's own parents, even if they were good ones, for there have been too many changes. What was right for their age is not necessarily right for today, and there are challenges they never had to confront (television is one of them).

A child's curiosity and absorption must be guided towards worthwhile interests.

The child's world begins in the home, and parents have a vital role to play in encouraging the development of meaningful interests, partly by example and partly by active effort. Drudgery in the home has been greatly reduced through improved technology. Adults no longer spend most of their time cutting wood, hauling water, preparing vegetables, weaving and sewing except by choice. If they feel pressed for time, it is because they have raised their standards and want to accomplish more. Parents' lives are less rigidly structured than they used to be, and so are their children's. But the new technology has heralded a new uncertainty about how best to organise the available time.

New focus on the home

The home has again become the focus for leisure pursuits. Interests, therefore, are more important than ever. Just as in the last century there was a trend to take activities out of the home (education, religion, medical care and industry all became relocated in specialised institutions outside the home), more recently the home has been accorded greater importance. Leisure interests have been brought back into the family sphere as families have acquired a whole new range of leisure tools—car, television, hi-fi and so on. Now father will probably spend more time on do-it-yourself activities in the home (partly for his own interest, partly because of the high cost of labour) instead perhaps of going to the pub or club to socialise. Also, the rise in material standards has made the home a more interesting place to be, a better centre for the potential development of children's, as well as parents', interests.

But this does not happen automatically. Father may be busy at carpentry, but if he excludes his children, or is impatient with their lack of skills, he may be doing the opposite of stimulating a potential interest. Or if he encourages his son but dismisses his daughter's interest in, say, the use of tools, he may establish in her a life-long inhibition. The same will happen if a boy's interest in housekeeping or cooking is discouraged. The fact that these biases fit traditional stereotypes may make it more difficult, but if parents wish to encourage interests to fit their child's bent, they will keep an open mind.

Too much prodding, or too little?

Parents' attitude to their children's interests is crucial. If they do too much for them, even out of devotion, they may fail to stimulate resourcefulness. If they do too little, they may deprive the child of the wherewithal to become competent. The middle ground seems to be safest: gradually involving the child in an interest, supporting it along the way as errors are made, increasingly encouraging it to do things on its own. It is not usually helpful to adopt a didactic attitude, seeking a lesson to tell the child about what is interesting in every experience that comes along. Rather, there is a way of expressing the interest through attitudes and actions. If parents take an interest (though not too much) in the child's experiences, the child may see for itself what is stimulating in them.

Somewhere between pushing children forward and holding them back—the magic mean for parents.

The anecdote of the father who gives his son a complicated train set for Christmas then sets it up and spends hours playing with it himself while his son plays with the boxes illustrates two points. One is that parenting requires a sensitivity to timing; there is no point giving a child a train set before he is ready for it. The other is that if a parent becomes too involved in an activity, the child may see it as intended principally for the parent's enjoyment rather than its own. This is particularly true if there is so much parental enthusiasm that the child construes it as pressure. In areas where the parent failed, or never got round to even trying, the child may seem to offer the parent a second chance. But pressure to excel at music, or tennis, or dramatics, can be a real turn-off for the child, especially if it is felt to be motivated by the parents' wish to compensate for their own failures in early life. Interests are best nurtured, not forced.

Television—boon or bane?

One of the issues likely to concern parents who want to raise children with developed interests is television. How much TV should we let children watch? How selective should we be? How should we handle the matter? Television can obviously be a tremendous boon to children (entertaining and educating them), to parents (as a child-minder among other things) and to elderly people (as a companion). Television is, without doubt, the most universal leisure activity, cutting across class boundaries: some 95 per cent of households own at least one set. More American houses have television sets than any other electrical appliance; many with televisions have no indoor plumbing. Yet TV can also be a worry. Many parents are anxious about their children's minds being warped by violent programmes, by the lure of consumerism in commercials. They worry that their children will become desensitised to the preciousness of human life, that passivity will become a lifestyle, and that television will detract from the development of various other interests such as reading, sports, etc.

The child may use television not only as an escape from unpleasant domestic and school chores and as a substitute for activity but also as a weapon in the struggle with parents. What if the child wants a set in its own room to watch more and more? Or if the child wants a bigger and better set because a friend has one? How about TV games and video-recorders? Is it good enough simply to say, 'We'll do it if we can afford it.'? Studies of family life indicate that parents' extreme anxieties are usually unfounded, but that to some extent effects depend on how the use of television is managed in the home.

Guidelines for viewing

Firstly, setting limits is important. Television is more likely to have harmful effects if children are allowed to watch any time they choose without any indication of what is acceptable. It is tempting, of course, to be easy-going, because unrestricted viewing frees parents from the pressures of child care and the struggles that come from disagreements. It is preferable, though, to be selective: some programmes are not only entertaining but contain elements of value in encouraging life interests in a broader context of activities of which TV is only one.

Secondly, participation is important. If at least some of the programmes are watched together, there is more chance that the experience will be used as an opportunity to stimulate interest. The content can be discussed, reactions to particular events or characters can be aired. The experience becomes a family experience, and parental values and interests can be improved. Research by Hilda Himmelweit and her colleagues has stressed the value of providing the child with standards by which to judge the material presented on TV. This set of standards is important for the child's general approach to learning as well as for its personality development and the control of emotions directly aroused by viewing.[7]

Parents and teachers

The interaction of family and school is of great importance in this phase of life. Parents and teachers are both concerned with the child's development. In some areas of life, and for some families, schools provide what the home does not, and the reverse is also true. But there is a good deal of overlap in their spheres of influence, which can lead to a sense either of sharing a task or of being at odds with one another. Sometimes teachers feel their mission is to save children from homes they regard as deprived or harmful. Sometimes parents feel *their* job is to provide correctives for the deficiencies of the school. Usually, the best arrangement is one of partnership, though it is often hard to arrive at in practice.

There are some interests that teachers can more easily stimulate in children. Parents can help develop a child's interest in music by arranging music lessons, selecting music programmes on radio or television, playing good music at home and visiting musical events. They cannot, usually, bring together an orchestra for the child to play in, whereas a school usually can. The same goes for other activities requiring large numbers of people, special skills or a lot of equipment. Even a large and talented family cannot cover the same range of interests as a school.

The need for diplomacy

A careful balance is desirable in the relationship between school and family. This is helped if both sides cultivate a kind of diplomacy in their relationships with each other, since both are important to the child's growth. If parents expect too much of teachers they may be disappointed, just as they will if they expect too little and try to do it all themselves. If each side acts as though the other does not exist, refusing to acknowledge the other's importance in the child's development, the child may be subject to conflict or confusion which could paralyse the emergence of interests.

Most studies of children's performance in school show that parental involvement is a powerful factor. Where parents show a genuine concern, the child tries to do better at school, and this is true of sports and hobbies as well as academic subjects. As we mentioned earlier, an excessive or spurious concern can be counterproductive, but too little can deaden the child's burgeoning enthusiasm. The key to healthy interests seems to lie in a balanced involvement.

3 Adolescence and the discovery of self

During the teenage years young people are involved in decisions which may be critical for their future lives. They have to decide whether to continue with further education, and if so what kind. If not, they must decide on the job or career they will pursue, or whether to reject the accepted patterns altogether.

They are also in the middle of reworking their relationships with their parents and family and with contemporaries of both sexes. They are very likely to be sexually active for the first time during this period.

A time of turbulence

Because so many new things are happening and the young person is beginning to be responsible for making important decisions, adolescence is often a time of turbulence—for everyone within striking distance (sometimes literally) as well as for the adolescent in question. It may be a time of experimentation, excitement, and the delights of creativity, whether it be writing poetry, playing music or playing about with motors. It is also a time when, because the young person is struggling to shake off the authority of parents or school teachers, there may be much quarrelling and answering back, storming out and slamming of doors, though the right is not necessarily all on one side. Often parents are at odds with each other as to the best way to handle these assertions of individuality. So rapid and complex are the changes during adolescence—the time between the beginning of puberty and full maturity and legal adulthood—that the teenage years are sometimes divided into sub-phases. In the earlier sub-phase, say 13 to 16, young people are mainly concerned with the push for independence from their parents, and the conflicts between dependence and independence that this involves. In the later sub-phase, say from 16 to 19, the emphasis is on the forging of a separate identity, distinct from those of the authority figures who have run their lives hitherto. This is an essential step for growth into full adulthood and the feeling that their interests are their own.[1]

Adolescence: Time to explore a wider world —and other people.

Refusal to be categorised

Adolescents' behaviour varies enormously, not just between one adolescent and another, but in the same adolescent from day to day, or even from moment to moment. Their attention often shifts from interest to interest; they may be highly volatile in mood and behaviour. When they describe their 'patterns' of activity, they may include activities they have pursued only once, or others they would like to pursue in the future, giving them an importance equal to their regular activities. This makes them extremely difficult to categorise, and indeed most adolescents deeply resent being categorised. Young people typically dislike other people organising or making plans for them—which is one of the factors that makes it hard for adults to give them guidance, especially those who most need it.

New models for old

Until adolescence, children are largely interacting with others in their families, in their neighbourhood and at school. But at adolescence a wider environment and many other influences come into play. Teenagers become conscious of the world beyond, and sometimes the people who have most influence on them are in fact quite remote—a pop idol, the leader of an exotic religious sect, or even a figure from a novel. It is common for young people to be strongly influenced by, for instance, characters in Tolkien or Dostoyevsky, or heroes portrayed in films like *Easy Rider* (their parents will remember *Catcher in the Rye* or *Rebel Without a Cause*). Less easy for parents to accept is identification with figures such as Sid Vicious or Malcolm X, or radical movements like the Symbionese Liberation Front or the Angry Brigade.

The importance of trust

The world of the teenager is not neatly divided into home, school and the beckoning outside world. Most will also learn to recognise people or things that cut across these compartments. For instance, 'people you can trust' or 'people who will back you up if you're in trouble'. Teenagers who have grown up with adults they have been able to trust are likely to form stable, trusting relationships with new people they meet, and, as importantly, be able to distinguish people who are worthy of trust from those who are not. Conversely, children who have grown up in an atmosphere of suspicion and anxiety will find it much more difficult to develop trusting relationships in adolescence, while the desperate wish to have someone to trust may precipitate unfortunate involvements in which they are exploited.

Teenagers are in some ways similar but in other ways inmensely different from each other. For some, adolescence will be the happiest time of their lives, for others the most wretched. Many seem to veer between ecstasy and misery in a way that is confusing to adults. Some are constantly busy and impatient, while others strike their parents as bone idle, staying in bed until lunchtime whenever they can, or endlessly 'mooching around' (though their minds and emotions may be a turmoil of activity).

They may be idealistic or selfish, or both at the same time; they may be aggressive or shy, arrogant or diffident. At times they want to be constantly stimulated, and at other times they seem to need to be bored; sometimes they hang around in cliques or gangs, sometimes they have to be alone. All or any part of this is perfectly normal—so long as we recognise and understand that it does not necessarily apply to all young people in the same way, or even at the same age, or to any particular young person all the time.

There are also sex differences, which are due to a blend of biological and cultural factors. Boys tend to be caught in conflicts between pressures to achieve and their wish to be esteemed for other kinds of activities in their peer groups (including sexual conquests). Girls are generally more concerned with the search for acceptance and security. There are signs in recent research on changes in boys' and girls' attitudes that these differences largely reflect cultural emphases.

The search for identity

Enormous variations are characteristic of this stage. But there is one common factor which will enable us to make some sense of the confusion. And that is that all adolescents share certain preoccupations, which have to do with the struggle to crystallise a *meaningful personal identity*.

The psychologist Erik Erikson has most clearly analysed this search for the answer to the question 'Who am I?'[2] The adolescent is trying out all kinds of possible identities, seeking to experience various roles, experimenting with different kinds of relationships, exploring his or her own mental and physical capacities. The outcome will be satisfactory if the chosen identity fits in with the real-life roles which are available—as a farmworker, say, or teacher, or mother—but there are likely to be signs of depression and despair, a sense of meaninglessness and low self-esteem, if the young person fails to find the answer to the question 'Who am I?' or if the favoured identity does not match any accessible social role or is not approved (for instance, if a young man with a conventional background decides to 'come out' as a homosexual).

One psychiatrist has described adolescence as 'a time of carefree wandering of the spirit through realms of fantasy and in pursuit of idealistic visions, but also of disillusionment and disgust with the world and the self'.[3] Anna Freud has interpreted the process as a 'saddening farewell to childhood, a renunciation of its pleasures and ties [and the] awakening and opening up of the joys and potentials of adulthood'.[4] Other psychoanalysts have portrayed adolescence as a continuous clash between 'progressive' and 'regressive' forces in the growth of the adult.

Adolescent issues

The preoccupation with finding their personal identity reveals itself in a number of typical adolescent *sub-preoccupations*, which are in turn expressed in *interests* characteristic in our society. These interests may be pursued through various *activities*, according to how readily available the activities are. A teenager with a love of animals will not find it easy to express on a council estate, where regulations forbid pets. And a passion for the sea is not easily satisfied if one lives far inland—at least not without a lot of money.

A number of sub-preoccupations, or issues, can be distinguished in adolescence.

Autonomy and independence

The young person wants to follow his or her own pursuits, preferably beyond the sight and control of parents and teachers. This may include doing things which are prohibited or even destructive or dangerous. Some theorists argue that a quasi-delinquent stage is normal for adolescents expressing their rebellion against authority. Highly negative attitudes towards the police, the economic and political system, the government and so on are typical, and often difficult for parents to handle calmly, because their own doubts and inhibitions may be stirred.

Since all young people must learn eventually to take responsibility for their own lives, the course that parents and others responsible for their growth usually try to take is to encourage as much autonomy as is consistent with responsibility, for themselves and others. Sometimes this requires considerable risk—hoping for the best. It also involves a readiness to be there to pick up the pieces when experiments fail, and to offer loving support when the brash, independent young person decides to come back into the nest for a little comforting.

Stimulation and boredom

Complaints about being bored are so frequent, as any parent knows, that it seems as if boredom is a necessary 'low' on the big dipper of excitement, and complaining is a kind of launching pad or recovery chamber for the next foray into the world. Most young people—again parents will testify—love (or at least don't mind) noise, speed, strobe lights, crowds, novelty, variety, experimenting with drink and drugs, and intense conversations. The charm of the motorbike lies partly in the mobility it offers, at reasonable expense, partly in its intoxicating speed, and partly, of course, in the opportunities it offers for making an unconscionable amount of noise and offending the neighbours . . .

Work in a wider world

A major aspect of the preoccupation with identity, and matching it with social roles, is naturally what to do with life as far as an occupation is concerned. It is not easy for the young to find out what adult work is like. We no longer live in a world where they routinely see and experience the work of their older relatives and neighbours. Choice is now much wider, but misconceptions are a frequent obstacle to finding the right job or career, and the thicket of examinations and qualifications can be daunting just at a time when personal explorations of the real world should be both more inviting and more adaptive for the next phase of life.

Adolescents who go on to further education have to make decisions about choice of subject. But their academic performance at school acts as a guide, and the decision is often not critical, since most colleges and universities make it possible for students to change courses if they have a change of heart. However, students are only postponing, in many cases, the decision of what work to do in the outside world. A false start at 22 or 23 may be a good deal more difficult to correct than a false start at 16 or 18. Of more importance in our view is the danger that they may miss opportunities to develop personal interests—either because of over-involvement in academic tasks or because of over-rebelliousness against them.

Sociability: the need for togetherness

Most young people, while often still conscious of the importance in their lives of their parents and other relatives, look to their contemporaries, their 'peer group', for many of their interests, for approval, for jokes, for gossip, games and competition. For girls, the 'best friend' of childhood may be replaced by the

In forging a new 'self' for themselves, adolescents work within the support-group of others of the same age.

'How about we pool our resources?'

confidante or boyfriend. For boys, this is the age of the street-corner gang, the football team or the terraces. Both sexes may gravitate to 'the scene'—the coffee bar, the dance hall, the pub.

Physical and sexual development

'The primary fact about adolescence,' writes social welfare professor Catherine Chilman, 'is that the young person becomes capable of reproduction.'[5] While giving full recognition to the social and cultural forces that shape adolescents' attitudes to sexuality, she notes that sex has a central role to play. A major preoccupation is what this role will be.

Adolescents are very involved with their developing bodies. Genital organs and breasts, body hair, muscles and so on have been developing for some time, and the urge to experience their bodies, to experiment sexually and learn about the feelings involved may be overpowering. Of all the characteristics of adolescence this is the one which has, at least in the past, aroused most tension between the young and their elders, although parents are learning to be more relaxed about it, particularly younger parents who were themselves brought up in a more permissive way.

Their affluence in recent years has made the young a ready target for commercial exploitation. Teenage preoccupations with appearance, identity, relationships, sex and self-expression have been catered to by a whole industry, including fashion, cosmetics, magazines, records and discos, often backed by sexually slanted advertising.

Intercourse and contraception

A welter of issues surrounds the whole question of sex. Contraception in the shape of the Pill and IUDs has reduced the toll of sexual permissiveness, but the most vulnerable, the very young, may remain out of reach of adequate sex education until it is too late: figures for illegitimate births, particularly among under-age girls, were rising alarmingly until not long ago. There is still considerable disagreement about the desirability of teaching young children about sex, and even more about whether contraceptives should be made available to adolescents as soon as they are fertile, and whether the legal age for sexual intercourse should be lowered. Some doctors feel it is medically inadvisable to put young women on the Pill or insert IUDs before their hormone balance has stabilised and their genital organs are fully grown, in late adolescence. The sheath and the cap, though medically preferable at this age, are less reliable alternatives, and often less acceptable to young users.[6]

Catherine Chilman points to the gaps in our knowledge on all these issues, and also to the importance of value judgements. She believes herself that casually performed 'recreational sex', however joyful and spontaneous, is not only risky (a factual statement) but produces the kind of person she does not value—one who is less likely to make responsible commitments to others with mutual trust. There is obviously room for argument here, as well as new information, because the issue is a lively and important one. An underdeveloped interest in sexuality can be as much of a handicap to achieving growth and satisfaction throughout life as its opposite.

Mental development

Many young people who have hitherto shown little interest in school work learn at this stage to enjoy exercising their minds: the 'late developer' is a common phenomenon. What is not so often recognised is that even non-academic young people enjoy using their brains, but sometimes in ways not usually catered for by schools and sometimes in ways that may actually be disapproved of. Often such young people can calculate odds in a betting shop with a high degree of accuracy; they know all the permutations of the football league table, and often have as good or better powers of human observation than their more intellectual fellows. The academic system of schooling has tended to separate intellectual and practical skills, pushing those who perform well in the former towards a purely academic regimen and disdaining the cultivation of other skills and interests which have been reserved for the less academic.

This emphasis on mental development may actually feed the interest in drug experiments, meditation and other 'mind-expanding' activities in academic-minded, middle class youth. It may also be behind the crafts revival by youth in revolt against the classical educational regime, and the appeal to youth in the '60s of social philosophers like Herbert Marcuse. Marcuse stresses the need for a better relationship between work and pleasure to combat the psychological impoverishment of what he terms 'one-dimensional man'.[7]

Experience of the environment

Young people's interest in a world outside their own school and neighbourhood may get closed off or inhibited as they grow up. In towns, they learn that it is dangerous to explore the streets; a country child is warned against the pitfalls of the city. While young people often seek new experiences, they may also be seen to turn up their noses at 'foreign' accents (which may be from the next county), 'funny' food and different habits.

Yet the instinct to learn about the unfamiliar at this age is a powerful one, and it has its part to play in the search for their own identity. The fresh-faced blonde country girl strolling down the street with the swarthy Middle-Easterner may reflect a search for her own identity as much as a rebellion against a straight-laced background, though her parents may wonder anxiously whether to intervene.

On the other hand, sometimes the young need to be encouraged to be adventurous in broadening their interests. Fortunately, school exchanges with foreign schools, which allow for this, are becoming more common. So are family swaps with foreign youngsters, and camping holidays with parents or friends, though city children often hate the country initially, finding it boring. The bicycle and motorbike have been liberating, sometimes hazardous, influences for the young of this century.

And the motor car, when they are able to use one, has offered them opportunities for an expanding range of interests.

Moral sensitivity

Acute sensitivity to what is right and wrong, just and unjust, is one of the most striking features of adolescence. In many, alas, it may never again in their lives be so acute—especially if there is no scope to translate it into an enduring interest which can be expressed in ordinary activities such as those organised by the voluntary social services.

Adolescents also become more alert to the discrepancy between what adults say and what they do—which leads to their readiness to demonstrate against this or that injustice. This belligerence may be irritating to adults, but it is as well to remember that they are often in the right, and in this sphere in particular it is foolish of the older generation to patronise them, treating them like children, or their views as misguided. Generosity of spirit and readiness to set the world to rights are valuable qualities, and the development of interests based on these impulses are of social value.

Striking a balance

Many young people become conscious that their preoccupations at this stage are confusing, and often contradictory. They may realise that their personal ideals will be hard to mesh with the realities likely to be available to them when they are grown up. They are keenly interested in joining the adult world: at the same time, they wish to *enjoy* life. But they can see for themselves that many adults do not enjoy life. We live in an age when enjoyment is still sometimes felt to be dangerously close to sin and (perhaps worse) to sap 'moral fibre' and the will to *produce*.

Rear-guard action—finding the balance between childhood fun and adult seriousness.

Also, much adult life is drudgery. Many young people feel that the lives of their elders have been stunted by the puritan ethic, or the capitalist system, or bourgeois values. Some feel the need to restore a balance by making an active effort either to enjoy their own lives more or to reform society. Neither is as easy as it sounds—and until they have worked through this stage and found a balance that suits them, many youngsters overreact and become hedonists or anarchists or rabid revolutionaries.

How teenagers are guided

Young people do not, of course, grow up in a vacuum. The way in which their essential preoccupations, discussed in the previous section, are expressed in interests and activities will very much depend on their environment—on the family in which they are growing up, on the school where they are developing their mental and physical abilities, and on the wider community within which both are set. Different influences surround each individual, but this general proposition is as true in Africa and India as it is in Europe or the Americas.

Family influences

Adolescence is usually a problem period in family life, and parents as well as children may find themselves in turmoil. We must emphasise once more that, as with all our generalisations, there is a good deal of variation. Even in the same family, one child is a problem, another easy; another child has its problems much later on; some seem to sail through adolescence without conspicuous trouble.

Childhood—a period of total dependence on adults.

Changes on both sides

This is a time of major change in lifestyle for both parties, parents as well as children. Although adolescents, even late adolescents, are not often entirely independent of their families, they *feel* that they no longer need their parents' care; certainly they do not need the same kind of care as they did when they were younger. Although most of them live at home at the beginning of adolescence, many will have left home by the end.

Further, where in childhood members of their families were the central figures in their lives, and other important figures, like teachers and other children, were to some extent controlled by the parents, in adolescence young people are beginning to choose other people to whom they wish to relate without much reference to their parents' views. The parents may not find this easy to tolerate. Most adolescents try to work out the best balance between attachment to their family—which is usually still extremely important—and growing attachments to others. Sometimes this balance is achieved only after a strong lurch to the other pole of independence.

At some time during adolescence young people are likely to earn their own money—first at part-time jobs, later at a full-time job. While many children will have been earning their own money for years, on newspaper rounds, on market stalls, running errands, at Saturday work in shops, even acting for TV or the stage, if only because of legal restrictions the money is unlikely to have amounted to much more than pocket money; if it *was* a large sum, for instance for film work, then it will have been paid over to their parents rather than to them. In many families a contribution to the cost of food and lodging is expected from earnings; and indeed there may be family pressure for the young person to leave school at the earliest possible moment.

Home—shelter or prison

Whether to live at home or not, and when to leave home, are issues that occupy the minds and emotions of many adolescents. For their parents, the issue is when and how to let go. The parental home is a shelter, saves money and may offer warm and supportive family relationships. But it is after all the place where the adolescent was, and is still referred to as, a child. Even if he or she is not closely supervised or organised any longer, being reminded of the child role is difficult to avoid and is the last thing most adolescents want. Even those who do want it realise that it may keep them from coming to terms with the world outside.

On the parents' side, there is great variation in the capacity to alter their relationships with the growing person to allow for his or her changing, and perhaps unwelcome, capacities and interests—including, of course, sexual interests. And not every home is warm and supportive. In many, the atmosphere may have become fraught during the phase of adolescence, and the loosening of the tie may be a relief to one and all.

Derek Miller and others who have written about adolescents in the family context have stressed the difficulties on both sides.[8] The adolescents have to give up the idealised view they held as children of their parents and their parents' values; they may also have to give up the gratifications—very real ones—of being looked after like a child. On their side the parents have to learn to relate to an independent-minded, often rebellious, sometimes seductive young person whose youth and lifestyle may make them uncomfortable or envious. This kind of conflict is one aspect of what is generally meant by the 'generation gap'.

Values come full circle

Each side often feels it has ceased to be able to communicate with the other. Adolescents feel the values of their parents are dull, boring, stupid, reactionary, or simply useless. Parents feel their children have thrown off everything that they themselves have invested their lives in. All this is a common experience at this stage. But many observers have noted that, if only the parents can tolerate it, the young people may eventually adopt very similar views—as their *own*, and not merely in order to please their parents. In fact, sociologists like S. N. Eisenstadt have stressed the vital importance of this uncomfortable process: it is the way in which the values of the community are reasserted from generation to generation, and it forms a necessary link for socio-cultural continuity.[9] Occasionally parents will express concern because their adolescent children have been 'too good', too quiet and conformist. The fear is for their later self-confidence and individuality.

Conflicts over family values are frequently echoed outside the family context, as when, for instance, pressures are exerted by students to get their college or university to do something they want. They may translate the generation gap they feel at home into the institutional sphere and take a more moral and personal tone with professors and administrators than purely organisational issues would seem to merit.

Handling problems

This sort of crisis often arouses very strong emotions in both adults and children. The emotions may be openly expressed or more or less hidden. The way in which they are dealt with may have critical and lasting effects on the young person's ability to develop satisfactory life interests. It can be very easy to damage a young person's capacity to grow into satisfactory adulthood. Parents vary greatly in how much they bring the problems into the open, and how well or badly they handle them. Parents are usually enjoined to express and communicate, because pent-up emotions and misunderstandings have made so much trouble. But sometimes at this stage being silent and waiting are important tactics. A word in the wrong place, however true, may be harmful.

The ideal mix

Many psychologists believe that the early family environment is at the root of severe adolescent problems when they develop. But whatever the origin, the management and further development of adolescents seems to be best served by a mixture of parental permissiveness and control, of warmth and firmness. One American psychiatric researcher, Lillian Kovar, restates a professional homily, that the good family is one which is good to go out from—encouraging new ventures and interests, not clinging on—but which creates the feeling that it is good to go back to.[10] All the same, from the point of view of the young person, a 'close' family may present as many problems as a troubled one. Breaking away from strong ties to find one's own identity may be more difficult. Sometimes it seems to have to be done explosively. Parents who are indifferent present fewer constrictions, but they also offer less rewarding relationships and therefore a less inviting atmosphere in which to develop personal interests and to return to when further support is needed.

We know much less than we would like about how parents and adolescents can develop shared interests, or mesh their different interests so that the family itself remains a good base for the adolescent. One point that seems to emerge from the Countryside Commission's research on family leisure is that at this stage a workable arrangement is for family members to travel to a destination together but to pursue separate interests and activities once there, perhaps returning together afterwards.

School influences

Education is a major avenue of opportunity for most young people. School is where interests may be aroused and cultivated. Even more important, young people's *resourcefulness* to develop their own interests can be fostered by education. But if schools are too oriented to academic or vocational ends, are too conscious of examinations and grades, they may stifle the awakening of individual interests except in those pupils whose own values are attuned to those of the school. And even for them, the sense of wonder, curiosity and delight that comes from the enjoyment of learning and developing skills may be lost if the learning or the skill is constantly being measured and tested, and there is too much pressure to achieve. Some progressive schools try to get round this problem by emphasising enjoyment and self-directed 'discovery' learning—but it is never easy to strike the right balance.

Factors of class

British research on how and why children do well at school, or fail to do well, has concentrated on the importance of their social class background. For instance the research of Basil Bernstein and his colleagues mentioned in Chapter 2 has analysed the difficulties experienced by pupils from working class homes because of the way their parents and neighbours speak. Working class language patterns are much more restricted, less 'elaborated' than the middle class ones which are normally used and required by teachers. And middle class interests are more highly valued by schools. A working class child may learn sports and hobbies at home very different from those favoured by the school, and may receive no encouragement from his family to read books. Where there are differences of values between home and school it is the child who experiences the conflicts.

If the values of the home and the school are different a child can find himself caught between them in 'no-mans-land'.

Michael Young and his colleagues have shown how children with middle class backgrounds are more likely to have parents whose values are in tune with the values of the school. Home and school are not at odds, which makes the learning process psychologically easier. It means that middle class children can more readily develop personal interests within the school context and sustain them outside. They are also less likely to leave school early and therefore to suffer the stunting in the development of interests associated with early school-leaving.[11]

Social class: a caution

It is important not to exaggerate the advantages to a child of being middle class, or the disadvantages of being working class, for there are too many variations. The family values which help a child to do well at school and to be enterprising and forward-looking are not exclusively middle class. Working class children may be free to develop interests not nurtured in schools. Many are pushed by their families towards higher education, and feel fortunate if they achieve it. On the other hand, there are plenty of middle class school children who are passive and pleasure-loving and live from day to day, perhaps rejecting their parents' pressure and not appreciating the advantages which have come so easily. Or they may have the development of their interests stunted almost as severely by parental pressure as the child whose family's interests are deficient or different. And there are some middle class families in which the children's development has dropped out of focus, because of career involvements, marital discord or other reasons.

But the present school system, with its emphasis on academic performances, does tend to place a higher value on its academic pupils than on those who do less well at conventional lessons. Since there is no reason why such pupils will *necessarily* be better adults or contribute more to society, this bias is one of the main arguments behind the move to 'deschool' education made familiar by Ivan Illich.[12] 'Deschooling' is a splendidly provocative idea; and others have called for more emphasis in schools on moral education, the development of what scientist Dennis Gabor has called an 'ethical quotient'.[13] (Some of these ideas turn out to be reminiscent of the old 'character-building' which was a major stock-in-trade of the great English 'public'—actually private—schools of the 19th and 20th centuries.)

Interests are paramount

We ourselves would stress the need for schools to encourage *resourcefulness* in young people. That does not mean we think the development of a moral or ethical sense is not important—it obviously is. But we believe it is just as important, and more attractive, to the young (who tend now to resent 'moralising') to encourage their interests, and to help them pursue at least some of those interests in depth. Of course schools already have activity groups which can channel the energy of children who are keen on sports, and most schools also have art classes, drama groups, music and singing lessons, woodwork and metalwork shops, cookery, opportunities for community service, and so on. But even the best schools could do more than they do. Apart from helping them to express the preoccupations of this stage of growing up, the encouragement of interests can lay practical foundations—in the shape of skills, know-how, confidence which will help them to confront the challenges of later years.

Having a goal in life: Interests established at school lay a foundation for meeting later challenges.

Indeed, we think that our society should regard the *encouragement of interests* at this stage as a major social investment. It will create dividends for the individual throughout his or her life, since skills and interests acquired at this age can be both useful and enjoyable later, and will help the process not only of growing up, but of growing through life and of growing old. It will also create dividends for society as a whole, because the development of interests is not only personally useful but provides links with others; ideally surplus energy is directed towards the community outside the family and place of work.

Community influences

The community influences the young deliberately—through church, the scouting movement, specialist clubs and more generally through advertising. It also influences simply by existing, by just being there. There is a culture and society outside our homes and schools that affects all that goes on inside—through political and economic events, through information and the media, through the provision of services and the exercise of controls. Young people want to know about what is outside there, how it works, how they fit into it; or, if they dislike it, how they could change it.

Some young people with the knowledge, the will and the means may explore far and wide—the Americas, the hippy trail to the East, across the Sahara, ot whatever—just to see what is there and to meet other young people on the same quest. Others will respond to community influences at a very local level; yet others to a world community and to world issues like nuclear disarmament or ecology or to the national community through politics or conservation.

Conformists and non-conformists

There are several ways of looking at young people's responses to their environment. The American sociologist David Matza provides one of the most useful: he distinguishes between 'conformist' and 'non-conformist' young people.[14] The conformists use the available facilities, at school, in clubs and at work, in ways that are socially approved in the adult world that provides them. The non-conformists, into which category many adolescents fall at least temporarily as part of the normal process of growing up, he describes as falling into three types: the bohemian, the delinquent and the radical. Explorations, particularly by the bohemian groups, often carry young people to the brink of, and beyond, what established society will accept. For a while the psychologist Timothy Leary lent a semi-respectability to the quest for ecstasy through mind-expanding drugs; and the Maharishi and his backers have brought the mystique of oriental religion to the quest for love and certainty through spiritual experience.

For the delinquent or near-delinquent, the 'brink' has to do with the laws relating to larceny, assault and battery, and disturbance of the peace. These are the young people who form gang sub-cultures like the Hell's Angels or skinheads or punk rockers—or a whole range of street gangs which emphasise daring, toughness and defiance in their flamboyant and aggressive flouting of authority.

The radicals are more intellectual and idealistic in inspiration, but they reject the liberal middle class ways of trying to realise these ideals. In Britain, the channels for expressing radical lifestyles outside the universities and professions include the radical or alternative press and a number of radical action groups such as the Socialist Workers' Party.

Instability as a way of life

Young people's activities are like a kaleidoscope, constantly shifting as their members move in and out from one group or activity to another. The difference between young people who conform and those who do not is often blurred, and any individual adolescent may switch confusingly from one pattern to another and back again. There are many anomalies and constant change.

This instability is caused partly by the growing-up process itself, and partly by the attitude of the wider community. Many social scientists have commented on the importance of society's attitudes since Margaret Mead's famous work in the 1930s and 1940s in which she showed that many of the problems our adolescents experience are caused by the fact that we provide a poorly defined phase between childhood and adulthood. In our industrial society, occupations call for lengthy schooling, and people are kept in a child-like role long past the age when they are physically mature. They then have a gap to leap between their child-like status as schoolchildren and adult status as workers.[15]

Adult attitudes

In a society as complex as our own, it is likely that some of the variation observed in adolescents' behaviour is due to variation in the attitudes of adults close to them. For instance, adults who regard the young as potentially out of control—threatening delinquency, licentiousness and anarchy—condemn the 'permissive society' and seek to strengthen control. Others, who may secretly envy the young as vital, creative, idealistic, uncorrupted by compromise and unbounded by vested interests, may encourage their audacious experiments with life. These different perceptions, often unconscious, find their way into popular stereotypes and writings about adolescence and affect the way adolescents are handled in specific situations.

Although early school-leaving leads to early economic independence, it can leave a vacuum of interests and goals.

Leaving school

School-leaving is a very mixed experience, particularly for those who leave early. The legal minimum in Britain is 16, but many effectively leave months, and in some cases years, earlier because they and their schools have virtually given each other up. Those who do leave early soon become financially independent. On the other hand, they tend to obtain jobs at the low end of the occupational totem pole, where they may remain more or less all the rest of their lives, with low pay and low self-esteem. When they leave school they may still be treated like children in their work organisation, which may make them feel resentful, since these are the very conditions they may have left school to escape. Further, away from work they may not be accepted in as many community activity groups as they would like, which may inhibit the development of new interests, or the continuation of such interests as sports or drama which school provided.

Here, in a nutshell, is the ordinary English adolescent's problem of shifting the channels he uses to express his interests from school to community:

> He may have come from a family that is perfectly good from the point of view of love and care but which may not have had much experience in relation to the contemporary range of associations which help to cultivate interests, and his family may not have taught him very much about how to relate to people who have other kinds of interests. His neighbourhood may not have provided many facilities. He has to find out about what there is, and try to guess what it would be like in them so as to match his own interests with what they offer. He has to make an approach, explain his interest to people who are ordinarily much older than himself and not necessarily keen to have youngsters in, particularly if they do not seem to be dressed right, or to talk right, or show that they are really keen. Their experiences of being rebuffed when exploring such situations may close them off for ever rather than developing the potential, very strong at this time, for awakening their latent interests and aspirations.

If the resentment such a young man already feels at work spills over into his leisure experiences, without his being able to find a way of expressing his interests, it may lead him into fighting 'the system' and even into delinquency. School and family are not enough to foster resourcefulness and interests. The wider community has a particularly important role to play in encouraging young people at a stage in their lives when they are especially vulnerable and potential for the growth of interests is particularly strong.

Delinquency can be a very real statement of frustration—an attack on a world which seems to offer no outlets for energy.

The lure of the bright lights ...

Commercial firms are all too ready to respond to the preoccupations of the young school-leaver, who is earning, sometimes good money, and has not yet incurred the heavy expenses of marriage and a home. This is the market of entertainment, fashion, music, motorbikes and sports, and the young will be drawn where these are provided. The city itself is a major magnet for the young. Many studies have shown that they tend to leave rural areas and small towns not just because the job opportunities are better in cities, but because cities are more fun.

In the large towns there is entertainment, stimulation, anonymity, acceptance into a wide variety of peer groups, and space to experiment in finding the answer to the question 'Who am I?' There is also callousness, exploitation, bad influences, loneliness, boredom and unfriendliness, which make for confusion, depression, fear and probably a few shocks to the young person's self-confidence. The real danger during this stage is that instead of developing a sense of identity out of his or her multifarious interests and widening experience, the young person will continue to be 'swamped' by them and conclude that life is meaningless and the world a dangerous and inhospitable place.

... and the need for meaning

It is crucial to emerge from this period with one's inner resources sufficiently developed to be able to turn one's interests into satisfying activities that can subsequently be pursued. Without this, there is the risk of increasing meaninglessness and poverty of interests later in life.

The Big City offers stimulation; or confusion. More traditional societies offer a stable framework for growth.

4 The decade of young adulthood

In the last chapter we focused on young people up to the time of leaving school. The age of leaving school, and the level of personal development reached by that time, is variable, but we took it that this adolescent phase was primarily concerned with the search for identity and the answer to the question 'Who am I?'

By the time they leave school, few people have actually found a permanent answer to the question 'Who am I?' Most people continue to seek the answer in one form or another throughout their lives, and continually revise their conception of what constitutes a satisfactory answer. But it is the principal preoccupation of adolescence. When they leave school, whatever their psychological and biological stage of maturity, young people are catapulted willy-nilly into more adult roles and a new set of preoccupations which will take them, very approximately the next decade or so to work through.

We took adolescence roughly to encompass the teens. We feel that the next phase, the early adult phase, starts at around the end of adolescence, say 19, and is likely to continue for about a decade until the early years of marriage or its equivalent, ordinarily in the late twenties. Thereafter, with marriage and child-rearing, we are into the establishment phase (which lasts until the mid-fifties). There are sub-phases in this timetable of psychosocial growth patterns, but they are not rigid, and both social change and individual variations must be taken into account.

Social options

People who continue with school or university after the minimum school-leaving age are likely to grow in a different way and at a different pace as they enter the young adult phase. Their resources for developing enduring interests are likely to be different from those of people who left school to take a job as soon as it was legal to do so, though the latter group may grow more rapidly into a specific range of adult interests and activities. Young people who continue in educational institutions may

Seal it with a kiss—
the beginning of
new responsibilities
and a new place
in the world.

experience a sense of shock when they eventually face the responsibilities of adult life.

Once out of school, young adults face several possibilities: going directly into work, travelling abroad, going into further education, living in 'anti-institution' groups and adopting an alternative lifestyle, or being faced with unemployment and thus starting adult life without an occupation, which provides the prime role identity of adulthood in our society. This is particularly true for men. Conventionally minded women place greater emphasis on marriage; but for both sexes marriage tends to come a little later. Men now marry for the first time on average at 25 in Britain, at 24 in the United States; women at 23 in Britain, at 21 in the United States.

These different ways of life can succeed each other or even co-exist in the same individual. For instance, it is quite common for a middle class school leaver of 18 to travel abroad for nine months before taking up a place at university; then after university to have a period on the dole, and/or living in a squat. A working class school leaver may try out a sequence of jobs—on an oil rig, in the army, as a lorry driver or factory worker—before settling down to an apprenticeship or a permanent job.

A different kind of discipline before settling into young adulthood.

Young adulthood is a life phase which has been studied very little outside universities. Soon after leaving school most people pass out of the sphere of the major juvenile agencies—school, juvenile courts, and the various youth services and youth employment agencies. Until recently young people under 21 were not listed on electoral registers. Even now, because they are constantly on the move between home and lodgings or hostel, or from rented bedsit to squat or commune and on again, they are often not registered. They have been difficult for social researchers to interview—with the major exception of students in various institutions of further education.

A need for relatedness

However, doing the best we can with the bits of information available, we can offer a general view of the preoccupations and interests of people in the young adult phase. We believe that the two principal preoccupations of young adults are the *search for an intimate relationship* or commitment and *identification with social institutions*. These two preoccupations tend to be channelled in four different sets of interests: interest in forming relationships with persons of the opposite sex (whether or not in marriage), occupational interests, parental and family interests, and friendship interests.

We examine the pursuits of these interests in four sub-groups of young adults—young conventionals living in a provincial town; students in higher education; the involuntarily unemployed; and young adults who have chosen to live for this period outside 'straight' society.

These sub-groups are only a partial cross-section of the whole young adult population, but data on them are available, and we have the impression that they cover a major part of the spectrum at this stage. One important group is 'straight' young adults in cities, who form an important group, but one which has not appealed much to researchers.

Intimacy and commitment

Normally a capacity for intimacy is developed by choosing and living with someone of the opposite sex. While this is usually within marriage, it increasingly occurs outside marriage—at least for a time. Many young adults do not wish to marry at all. Some prefer partners of the same sex, or group sex, or living together as man and wife but without legal formalties. These choices are no longer condemned, as they used to be, as immature or immoral. We regard them as variant patterns which are often favoured at this stage of life. Finally, some young adults can relate more intimately and commit themselves more easily to the institution itself, rather than to the people involved. Thus there are people for whom it is important simply to be married, and not so important to have a close intimate relationship with husband or wife.

Just which institutions people focus on in young adulthood varies with sex, class, lifestyle, early influences, personal history, the society in which he or she lives, and so on. For example, although women now work outside the home more than ever before, the social prejudice against women having serious careers is still so strong that most women identify less with their occupation than do most men. Some young women do, of course, like some men, identify strongly with their work. But for women generally marriage still tends to be the primary institution for resolving their preoccupation with social identity, while men still identify primarily with an occupation.

In recent years there has been a significant change in what is expected by society. It used to be that commitments made at this stage—whether in marriage, or in a particular career like the Civil Service, or a family business—were commitments one was stuck with for life. That has changed. There is much greater acceptance now that people may change their interests, and with them their careers. Or circumstances may change and the need to grow in new directions may be thrust upon them.

Links with social institutions

It is still important for the development of young adults that they commit themselves to a set of social institutions in which they can take roles—a person, an occupation, a community—but not necessarily expect that they will be immutable, until death or retirement. While the lack of a career at all may still cause raised eyebrows, the concept of multiple careers is much more acceptable than it once was, and may even be essential if one is to adapt to real life changes. Divorce figures show that an increasing proportion of the population still favour marriage as an institution, albeit with a high turnover.

Young adulthood is *par excellence* the age of role rehearsals, in contrast with the more tentative exploration of the preceding stage. Some flexibility is essential, as the try-outs may fail, and in any case the capacity to readjust is likely to be an important one to cultivate as a lifelong resource. But the preoccupation with *commitment* gains in importance as the underlying ingredient of experience at this stage.

Small-town conformists

It is in small towns that conventional ways of life are most firmly established. In a world like a goldfish bowl where everyone knows everyone and most of what you do is observed and commented upon, the sanctions of public opinion are powerful.

Studies by sociologist Diana Leonard in Swansea in the late 1960s have given us an excellent picture of the preoccupations of young working class adults in Swansea, in South Wales which, though not strictly a small town, can be said to reflect small-town ways of living and thinking.[1] Many middle class people, too, will recognise this picture as true of themselves at the same stage of life.

These studies show that a main interest of young adults in Swansea is courtship and marriage for girls, getting a job and 'perhaps marrying' for boys. As early as twelve to 14, both sexes show an interest in sex which may deepen into love.

The first experiments are over—now is the time when a young man's (and woman's) fancy turns to love and commitment.

The importance of courtship

Young Swansea women are likely to have embarked on these more committed relationships during their last year or two at school. The young men have 'fooled around' with girls, but tend to wait until they are 17 or 18 before beginning anything like a serious courtship. After one or two 'steady' relationships, the serious business of courting begins. The average age of formal engagement in Swansea in 1968 was 19 for young women and 21 for young men. Marriage follows a year or so later, and the first baby arrives within the next two or three years. Middle class young people, partly because they are more likely to go on to further education, will probably embark on serious courtship and marriage two or three years later.

Public milestones

During the early stage of their heterosexual career, ordinarily beginning in adolescence, both sexes tend to spend their spare time hanging around on street corners, in youth clubs, coffee bars and recreation grounds with other young people of the same age. They seize their chances of 'picking up' a member of the opposite sex, 'chatting them up', offering a smoke or a drink. Starting these grown-up pastimes is very important for young people's views of themselves as adults. Boys need to be accepted at a pub, to get drunk (and be seen to get drunk), make and boast about conquests, and girls need to be seen to have a boyfriend. To the extent that these are ritualised, publicly recognised milestones, they are like what anthropologists call *rites de passage.*

The first step: formal dating

Diana Leonard's study confirms the persistence in contemporary small town culture of such traditional patterns and sequences. Dating starts with acceptable activities like going to the cinema or a dance, then progresses to less clearly specified destinations and activities, like going to listen to records in each other's houses or going for a drive, and, at a more advanced stage, visiting a local lovers' lane.

Young adults who intend to go on to further education have less time and money for formal dating activities like going out to a coffee bar or cinema than those who intend to leave school at the earliest possible moment. The latter have no homework to do and have begun to earn money to finance their dates. Young people who go on to further education may pride themselves on being economically self-sufficient, thanks to grants and part-time jobs, but the development of their leisure interests is likely to be tied up with the activities surrounding an academic institution—reading, discussion, lectures, political meetings, art exhibitions, meetings of various academic societies and interest groups.

After leaving school, young men who are earning are probably less under the thumb of their parents (though the parents may complain that their young are treating their home 'like a hotel'). They continue with the kinds of masculine pursuits they developed at school—football, darts, motor cycling or whatever—but they will possibly ask young women along too.

The young woman's shrinking world

Young women may tend to feel the discontinuity from school to work more sharply. Parental supervision may continue, but in contrast to the young man they tend to give up the kind of sporting activities they enjoyed at school. This is partly because there are fewer sports facilities for women than for men and partly because they now regard sports as childish or unfeminine. They give up youth clubs because the boys who go there are too young. In any case, youth clubs do not usually cater for courting interests. We sometimes get the impression from studies sponsored by youth clubs that young people who leave the clubs because they have started courting are in some way 'deviant'.

Young women derive prestige from finding suitable, usually older, boyfriends who will take them out and accompany them to places they feel they could not go to alone. With any luck the young man may pay for their entertainment as well.

After leaving school, a young woman usually likes to continue dancing as an activity, but whether she actually goes dancing or not depends on whether she has a boyfriend, and whether he likes it. She can go with girlfriends, but if a relationship with a boyfriend develops and becomes more serious, he may object to

When schooldays are over, many women's activities centre around their men—directly, or indirectly.

her going to dances. He, on the other hand, may be less willing to give up his evenings in the pub with his friends. The young man may not mind if she and the other girls of the group come along, not drinking as much, but just sitting while he and his mates drink, play darts and tell stories. But he won't like her going separately to dances and places where she may meet other males. The young woman deals with the situation by strengthening her relationships with female relatives—going shopping with her mother, visiting her married sisters, and so on. This does not threaten the developing relationship with her boyfriend and serves to develop interests and competence in homemaking skills which will help her grow into the anticipated roles.

The second step: engagement

As casual dates change to steady dates, the young couple meet each other's parents and move gradually towards getting engaged. They start to spend more time at home (usually at the girl's home, unless she does not get on with her parents or there are too many younger children), listening to records, watching TV, or 'courting' in the front parlour (the best room, ordinarily reserved for social occasions and special events like funerals). They may start becoming more like friends to one or other set of parents—and even though one of the young couple may begin to be bored by the time they have been going steady for two or three years, the relationship may, for this as well as more obvious reasons, be extremely difficult to break.

Among the conventionally minded young adults of the kind we are describing—still more prevalent in the world than urban sophisticates may think—premarital intercourse is frowned on, though these seriously courting young couples are often left alone when the parents go to bed. Though they may already have started saving a little for marriage, serious saving only starts with the formal engagement. The boy then works long hours of overtime, drops out of his leisure pursuits such as drinking at the pub, having only an occasional outing with his fiancée.

The bride-to-be stays mostly at home or with other engaged couples, or visits the boyfriend's parents. There are interminable discussions about the wedding, and Saturday afternoons are spent looking at furniture, and then looking for somewhere to live. When they have found a place, they spend their weekends decorating it. This is a period of intense togetherness—and their relationship is very close at this time. Meanwhile they are being accepted into each other's adult world:

> 'She (his mother) no longer talks *to* me about "our Tommy"—she talks *about* me as "our Eileen", and she shows me photographs and talks about what he was like when he was little. Once we were engaged they trusted me to look after the shop! And they talked about family matters in front of me.'

Thus a young woman narrows her range of interests to those which are important for courtship and marriage. She gives up her pre-engagement activities, because they involve going with her girlfriends to places where there are unattached men. In any case, she no longer needs to be interested in other men. Her activities centre more and more on her relatives, and her friends are usually one or two other engaged or just-married girls on whom she may drop in for a chat (and a preview of the lifestyle to come). She will also be seeing the couples with whom she and her fiancé go out.

The third step: marriage

The pattern which will continue after marriage is established early. The new bride's behaviour in concentrating on home-making shows that she accepts that a woman's place is in the home, unless her husband takes her out of it. Her outside interests have been cut off quite radically, and with them her resources to cope with the troubles and challenges that the future may bring. She stops developing new outside interests and turns her attention to domestic ones. Her job is not important to her except as a source of savings for the future. She gives no thought to the fact that once her future children are mobile she is more likely than not to return to work. If she does consider returning to work, her feeling tends to be that her husband would not like it; and she is likely to be right. (There are some signs, however, that this pattern may be changing.)

Students: time out of life

Further studies—for some, a breathing-space in which to continue exploring self and society without too much outside pressure.

Full-time students comprise a substantial minority among young adults all over the developed world. In Britain, about 20 per cent of those aged 18 to 21 are students, and in the USA the figure is higher still. Even in countries where students are less numerous, they are likely to be an extremely important sector of the population.

Students in institutions of higher education are in a position to develop a wide range of interests. They have time, opportunities and external encouragement to develop resourcefulness. This is true not only of their academic work, but of all their time and activities. The traditional ideal of a student's life allows for the development of ideas and skills through informal discussion with staff and fellow students, exploring, as well as specialist academic subjects, the wider fields of religion, politics, sex, emotions, the arts, social issues and so on. And there is likely to be a continuation of interest in the body (expressed in sports, yoga and sex) as well as in the intellect.

A liberal education?

Developing skills in argument, reading to find evidence to support a particular point of view, getting to know many different kinds of people and lifestyles, experimenting with new food and drink, taking part in sports or music or drama, are not only relevant to a future occupation, but to making one's way in life according to the prevailing ideas of a liberal education. Peter

Marris wrote, in his study of British higher education in the 1960s:

> Most people who have faith in a university believe that (it) can give (a liberal) education, and that this is its particular justification. The ideal implies ... the development of a generalised rational understanding both from the courses themselves and, equally, the social environment in which the student learns. For him university is not so much an institution as three or four years of his life when living away from home, making friends, falling in love or realising his religious convictions may be as important as studying for a degree.[2]

However, this ideal is not as widespread as it might be. At many universities and other further education institutions, getting a degree or other qualification is of overriding importance; at others, students do not live in halls of residence but continue to live at home, in part under their parents' control. Nor is the ideal even as generally desired at it once was.

Where the research is focused

Of all young adults, most is known about university students. (Less is known about students in specialist colleges like agricultural institutes and art and drama schools.) A good deal of the research tends to focus on things like aptitude testing, teaching methods, student 'wastage' and performance (which are useful to those responsible for financing further education), and not on how the students actually develop and grow as people. Students are encouraged to take a year off for work and travel, hopefully to broaden their horizons and to encourage resourcefulness, but this experience, like the educational experience itself, is not well described as yet.

Peter Marris's study *The Experience of Higher Education* is a wide-ranging analysis of what it means in the lives of young people to spend three or four years at an institution of higher education. He examined three universities and a College of Advanced Technology in the early 1960s from the point of view of their students. This study gives us some insights which are probably valid still, though there have been many changes (the old technical colleges now have much higher academic status, for instance).

Britain's two-tier system

The students Marris studied rarely stopped to consider what further education potentially provides. Most students in British universities have accepted the logic that it follows from their success at school they they should proceed to higher education. Many are simply going up the academic ladder, and doing what is expected of them. They do an honours degree at university if they are judged to have the ability; they go to what is considered a 'lesser institution' if they do not. They rarely go to an alternative institution because they want what it has to offer (even if what it offers is more suitable for their needs than what a university offers).

End of a romantic dream

Because of the pressure to get good examination grades at school and the assumption that university is the goal, many students arrive at college and 'seem at first to wait passively for some inarticulate but great fulfilment'. Many become disenchanted—academically and socially—when their romantic dreams of 'gaiety, freedom, intellectual excitement and graceful surroundings crumble'. Further, they are so conditioned by the spoon-fed way they learned at school that they do not know how to adapt to learning on their own and relying on their own initiative to make the most of their opportunities. By the time they do, their final exams may be almost upon them. Those who have developed a clearer sense of their own autonomous identity, and have cultivated a sense of resourcefulness, have a better chance of finding and using the opportunities available in university settings.

In Marris's study, those who actively chose a lesser institution such as a technical college were less disillusioned, because they expected less. However, those who went to such institutions because they failed university entrance remained highly critical of the cultural deficiencies in their second-choice institutions.

College: social necessity . . .

Most students continue to study the subjects they were best at at school. But some subjects, like economics, law, medicine and the social sciences, are seen as possible new subjects to take up. A sizeable proportion of students switch from pure to applied sciences, adopting a more 'calculating' attitude about the usefulness of their studies. This is more a tendency—perhaps more necessary—among middle class students. Marris compares the middle class student, who 'sees his university career primarily as a means of qualifying for an occupation similar in status to his father's and . . . feels his parents to have been a more important influence . . . than his school', with the working class student who 'sees the university more as the final prize in the competition for education, whose vocational usefulness he takes for granted. . . . Neither student has the social or intellectual opportunities of the university uppermost in his mind.'

. . . or social advancement

Marris does not discuss women students in the same way. We know from other research that women, irrespective of class background, tend more to read arts or social sciences. Like some working class male students, they often see coming to university as an end in itself. For many women, the social side—finding a husband of similar status—may also be important. But here there is a tricky point in that women narrow their range of eligible partners by obtaining higher education more than do men. Men bring their wives up to their own social status even if they are less educated. Educated women cannot as readily do this for their husbands, so they must seek a husband from a narrowing range of eligibles.

In the United States, research has come up with very similar findings. For many middle class young people, college has been accepted as a social necessity. For working class youth it tends more to be seen as a means of social advancement in which, as sociologist Joseph Kahl[3] showed, children of the more dissatisfied working class parents were pressed to go on to further education while children of their more contented counterparts received less encouragement. Not only the actual education or vocational training are involved, but also adopting a certain style of life and developing a wide range of personal interests.

No time to read

Yet most of Marris's students did not feel that their higher education had contributed much to the development of their general interests:

> Only a fifth of the students at each university had attended any lecture outside their course during the term. . . . It seems to be rare for a student anywhere to attend lectures of another course; he finds time, if at all, only for the open lectures. Nor is there much leisure for general reading. Altogether, a quarter of the scientists had not opened a book at all during the term, apart from their studies, and another quarter had read only light fiction, or motor racing manuals, while 15 per cent of arts students had read nothing and eight per cent merely light entertainment. Outside Cambridge (University), only around a fifth had found time for more than a couple of serious books.

Studies in the USA have shown similar overall patterns. Psychiatrist John Summerskill[4] has reviewed available research on dropouts from college and found that the largest proportion typically attributed dropping out to 'lack of interest'. He writes: 'One recurring description of dropouts runs as follows: The dropouts were . . . "in College because of various motives which, however, did not include a desire to study".' Those with vocational motives are more likely *not* to drop out, but there is no simple relationship between personal growth and staying or leaving. Though many reports of clinicians studying dropouts emphasise their neurotic problems, John Summerskill notes that the students themselves do not usually share this view.

Extra-curricular lectures and reading are of course only part of a general education—if one were to include social life, going to theatres and cinemas and exhibitions, playing games or other sports, or taking part in politics or whatever, many students would in fact be considered to be getting much more of a general education than Marris implies. And those activities are probably more developed in British univeristy communities than they were a decade ago. In the United States, a number of studies, such as that by psychiatrist Benson Snyder,[5] have paid more attention to what is called the 'hidden curriculum', often more important for growth than the formal one.

The main frustration reported in the British study, particularly by science students, was lack of time. Marris felt that even if their academic work were reduced and more time made available, most students would probably spend it on their special subject, because getting a good grade in their degree is so important for their future careers.

It is also probably easier for arts students to widen their interests at college than for science students. This is not just because they have less assigned work—on the contrary. It is, rather, because cultural interests—the arts, religion, politics and so on—are easier for arts students to relate to their course of study, and may even add to their qualifications and be useful in their future careers. In other words, they have an interest in widening their interests.

Living arrangements make a huge difference

There has been a lot of research on the importance of residence in people's experience of university, but it is very difficult to disentangle its significance. To be an undergraduate at Cambridge is potentially very 'rich' culturally; yet it is known that many undergraduates there feel very lonely, and those who live not in college but in 'digs' can find a landlady's room even more depressing than a box-like bedsitter in a tower block. A flat shared with other students who are stimulating, friendly and supportive in a less favoured university would seem more conducive to the development of interests.

The experience of living in a mixed residential college is likely to have a very different impact on students. While this living arrangement is still not closely evaluated, our impression is that it allows for the growth of the whole person, particularly important as higher education spreads to more people and for longer periods of life. The lifestyle is less artificially monastic. In the USA over ten per cent of students marry while still at university, and a much larger proportion live as married. There is no indication that this is deleterious to academic performance, and some that it helps.

An unreal world

The university experience has elements of a tribal initiation ceremony on a grand scale. Marris writes:

> A community of students . . . draws together men and women of a similar age, ability and interests, making them aware of each other as the academically privileged representatives of their generation. Their years at university are an initiation into the elite of their society, and the sequestration, the ceremonies of graduation, recall the rites through which the age grades of some African societies traditionally pass. . . . Undergraduates are estranged from their past and their future, within a community more diverse in opinion and background than any they have known, or will know again, and yet extraordinarily homogeneous. This is the outstanding attraction of university life, and also the source of a pervasive anxiety.

Many students feel anxious because they are in limbo. In this respect it resembles a period of national service in the army.

They feel isolated in a closed, unreal, artificial community, living a life removed from the mainstream of their community. They do not know where they will find a place in the mainstream, and they are unsure about whether any place they can visualise will be congenial. Some researchers have suggested that this kind of very fundamental anxiety was an important factor in the world-wide student unrest which began in the late 1960s. It may contribute to high student dropout rates in the 1970s and 80s.

The fruits of unrest

Marris was writing before then, and there is no doubt that, although only a minority of students were or are extremists either in word or in deed, and although as we write there is a new mood of conservatism among students, at least in the US and Britain, the radical action and rebelliousness of 1968 onwards had a powerful impact on universities.

The universities themselves have become more democratic and tolerant: students have much more say in what their syllabuses should contain, and even what kind of teachers they should have, and what kind of rules and regulations there should be. Staff have learned to take for granted that the students will have sexual relations, and even live together—which would have been unthinkable in many colleges even as recently as 20 years ago. The transition period was not easy: the staff, taken by surprise, did not know whether these new-style students were simply tiresome adolescents grown older and noisier, or dangerous enemies of the social order, perhaps tools of others with sinister purposes. Nor did they know whether to treat students

The 'student revolution'—a challenge for change and growth, for both people and institutions.

who trespassed, destroyed property, banned dissent or interrupted teaching as criminals or delinquents.

Were the cultural revolutions of the USA, Great Britain and France as counterproductive as China's? Was it the generation gap writ large? Like insecure parents, university faculties and administrations were deeply split and disturbed over the issues raised by their students. Universities have changed, and fewer students are as aggressively rebellious as they used to be. Both the individuals concerned and society have learned something about the roots of disturbance in young people, and the ways in which their actions can affect social institutions, but many of the sources of disturbance remain.

Vacation work: a link with reality

From the point of view of *personal* as distinct from intellectual growth, one problem students continue to experience is the isolation of universities from the world of politics and public affairs. They have lacked opportunities to test their abstract ideas in the 'real world'. But students now take paid and other outside employment during their years at university far more than they used to. Working one's way though college has been common in America for a long time, but it is only recently that British students have taken to working for pay, especially during the long summer vacation, spurred by the fact that living costs have risen so much more rapidly than student grants. Nowadays, three quarters of students take summer jobs, and others work for experience.

Some tutors regard this lack of study during the long vacation with dismay, but many students, even very academically minded ones, trade their chances of a First Class degree—which they know affects job chances—for a good Second. They feel that this is good enough for most careers and that a wider experience of the world, either paid work or unpaid travel abroad, will serve them in another way, broadening their interests and helping them to grow as people. Others, even more troubled by the remoteness of universities from the pressing concerns of the community, drop out altogether—even if their academic records are good. Many American universities encourage such schemes in the form of a 'junior year abroad'. The informal educational aspects of living in another country are recognised in such programmes.

The problem of loneliness

However, social isolation remains a problem for many students. One researcher found, in a study of a London science department, that the staff, who were selected on academic grounds, did not have the skills needed to help their students develop the wider interests that would help them to live their lives fully, nor in many instances did they feel that this should be their proper function.[6] Students who were lonely and uncertain of themselves remained lonely and uncertain, and were not helped to develop as people—to grow into adulthood. Low student morale, apathy, neurotic complaints, suicides, under-performing and high wastage remain a problem nearly everywhere, and we feel that the argument sometimes offered that the really capable ones survive is not good enough. Society needs to bring out the best in *all* its young people, not just a hardy few, and enable as many as possible to enjoy themselves as people, rather than only as skilled performers. This value position applies to all situations in which young people develop, non-students as well as students. But the failure of young people who are potentially the most highly skilled and productive to society as a whole is particularly poignant, for they have been led, and have a right, to expect a good deal more.

The young unemployed

People in modern industrial societies tend to think of work as not only a good thing, but *morally* good.

These days, even those with every privilege and advantage will also be expected to work.

The situation for women is also moving in the same direction. Whereas women before the Second World War tended to leave their job on marrying, most now continue to work, at least until they have children, whatever their financial resources. Whether or not one needs it, a job provides money; it allows for some degree of self-expression, structures a large part of one's time, gives purpose and direction to one's life, and broadens one's social horizons. People are 'placed' socially by the work they do, so work also gives status.

On the other hand, not everyone has a personal commitment to their work. Many work at jobs they feel have little social value, and they feel that they have little discretion or control over what they do. Others actively hate their work, or the people they work with, find it dehumanising, feel exploited or manipulated, or find that it causes them intolerable anxiety and stress.

Envy, suspicion, sympathy

One might think that such people would welcome unemployment as a relief from a noxious or undesirable situation. But, in fact, most people have mixed feelings about being unemployed. At first it may feel like having a long holiday; then things begin to become uncomfortable—particularly after the initial spurt of activity of looking for a job is over. Others may begin to ask themselves whether they are genuinely looking for work, or looking for work they are not fitted for. Finally, there may be hostility: are they work-shy, or fiddling the system to get income without paying tax while others foot the bill? Then there may be resignation, often with a considerable drop in self-esteem. Though it is more widely recognised now that the unemployed are often victims of circumstances beyond their control, and people say 'There but for the grace of God go I', it is rarely an easy situation to grow in.

The right to work

The unemployed do not usually welcome unemployment. The idea of a 'right to work' is deeply ingrained in the minds of workers as part of a struggle to escape from being exploited by a system that dehumanises people and discards them when it suits. Much less widely appreciated is the idea that *occupation* is the important thing—independent of economic motives. If income is maintained by the state or the union or an insurance policy or one's spouse, the problems of being meaningfully occupied could be dealt with separately. But this requires a new definition of the situation, and of the potentials in it for developing one's interests. In a word, it requires a new kind of resourcefulness.

Victims without a voice

For young people who are unemployed there are special problems. There is widespread anxiety, both among the young and on their behalf. In Britain in 1974, 50,000 were still unemployed six months after leaving school. In January 1978 the figure was 240,000. And often it was those who could afford it least who were most vulnerable, like blacks and single parents. Since adult unemployment rates are much higher among the unskilled than for the skilled (five times higher in the US) school leavers, lacking training or references, are particularly hard-hit in times of recession.

Official statistics of unemployment are nearly always on the low side. Many young people do not register for work at employment exchanges, perhaps feeling unprepared to deal with bureaucratic systems of claims, and so do not draw the benefits to which they are legally entitled. Consequently, they are 'socially invisible', and except where there is fear of delinquency or a backlash against discrimination (as in the case of black youth) there is little explicit concern. They are no longer at school and have not yet reached the world of work, with its unions and insurance contributions; they are therefore more difficult to keep track of and may be felt to be well enough looked after still in their parental homes. Their elders, feeling insecure about the possibility of being undercut or displaced, collude in the silence. The young unemployed are also difficult to talk to, are not very articulate (so they do not form a ready pressure group), and are suspicious of people asking questions about how they are making out financially (so there is little research).

The graduate pool

University graduates also face unemployment, but they are more visible socially and there is the feeling that the community has made an investment in their education which should not be wasted. In Great Britain in 1966 less than three per cent of graduates had not found a job by the end of the year (five per cent were unaccounted for), but in 1977 17 per cent of new graduates were not in employment, despite the efforts of placement services.

In the United States, where a higher proportion of individuals get university education—though more at their own expense—the issues are seen somewhat differently. Does the American Dream of unlimited upward mobility through increased education pay off? If not, what is wrong? and what *would* pay off? Does education *unfit* some people for jobs?

When the holiday feeling wears off

Initially, unemployment feels like a holiday, but it soon becomes boring, and the feeling builds up of having no place in life. The young person looks for jobs quite energetically to begin with, but after a succession of refusals may begin to despair. In some cases experience will confirm earlier attitudes about the system which may make it difficult ever to hold down a job. Others may find casual work but lose their jobs when the time comes for the firm to make a more permanent commitment. Being young, they are liable to become redundant under the rule of last in, first out. They leave work feeling exploited or a personal failure because they tried their best to no avail.

How does an unemployed young adult fill the day? The English sociologist Dennis Marsden[7] talked to a number in the heavy industrial area of North-East England, and concluded that they did not use their time very constructively from the point of view of developing interests which could serve their own growth in later jobs or phases of life. Most hung around their homes, becoming more and more bored and starved for company. A permanent diet of transistor radios, records and comics simply fed their boredom:

> The phrase being 'stuck in the house all day' expressed very clearly the sense of having no work or substitute work and no desire . . . to be part of the home world of women and children. And this feeling was voiced most acutely by (young people) who, almost with one voice, described their days of unemployment as 'crap', 'boredom' or 'murder'.

'Oh crap! Like you're in the house on a Monday, on a Tuesday, Wednesday you gang (all together) go down the dole. On a Thursday to the dole to sign . . . just signed, went back home, and that was it. I was in till the following Thursday.'

'Oh, it's boring. I used to go and play football or something like that, sit about the house and play me guitar, and I just got fed up. Me mother was on at us. She was always saying, "Get out and try and get a job." You can hardly wonder you were made depressed when you got turned down.'

Creeping demoralisation

Nothing could more clearly illustrate the loss of morale and identity in young unemployed people suffering continued rebuffs from employers and censorious remarks from family and neighbours. They may even be urged by family, employers and Labour Exchange to alter their painfully won view of themselves, and to change their ideas about the kind of job they want and the wage they expect to be getting. It can be painful to be asked questions by acquaintances and strangers, however well-meaning: 'You're in a pub, and inevitably the question comes up, "What do you do?", and if you say you're unemployed they don't want to know, they just turn away.' This is partly a matter of the young person having no work or shared experiences to discuss, but also that he is thought to be unable to take his turn buying a round of drinks. And there is a certain stigma attached to being unemployed. It is still suspected that it may be because there is something wrong with him as an individual.

The lack of a job around which to organise one's day is important. Many unemployed find their biological rhythms disturbed: they are wakeful at night and tired during the day. Some spend a lot of time in bed or become apathetic, even losing interest in previous hobbies. Marsden's young people mentioned growing laziness as a worry—they were themselves afraid that they were losing the will to work and becoming unemployable, a fear shared by their parents. This can lead to the ruin of previously harmonious family relationships.

Short-term solutions

Some unemployed people show resourcefulness by making work-like activity for themselves. This is work or occupation in the social psychological sense, even if it is not employment in the sense of being economically remunerative. You can say that you are working on building a shed or a boat, or with a youth club, and this will be seen, felt and talked about with similar interest and involvement as any kind of job, even if it does not provide money. But it is not usually an adequate permanent solution.

One man who had been unemployed for several years did a lot of house decorating for a time. But his father-in-law's sarcasm drove him out, and he spent all his days in a hut on an allotment with other unemployed friends. There, unemployment was the norm. Others do handicrafts or window-cleaning—not as a full-time job, but informally to supplement their dole money. They may even adopt a pseudo-occupational identity: one young man always wore a British Road Services jacket to indicate why he was walking around the housing estate in the middle of the day.

To be able to find a meaning for their lives accounts for the enthusiasm which many unemployed young people express for doing paid community service. In Britain, unemployed young people are recruited by local authorities to do all kinds of useful work, from decorating old people's homes and digging up their gardens to helping on archaeological excavations or doing surveys of local plant life. It can only be short-term, and wages are low, but it feels 'better than being on the dole'.

Other ways out

Some young unemployed get psychological and other support from their peers. They gang together in cliques, and go in for a bit of petty thieving to supplement the dole. Or the occasional young unemployed gets taken up by a group of students, who accept him as one of themselves, and open his eyes to another world. He may or may not collect his dole, but he can probably find a crash pad in a squat or the corner of someone's flat, cadge enough food and drink to stay alive, do a bit of amateur thieving or push hash and be taken along on outings and to pop festivals and parties. He will feel part of the 'scene', perhaps develop an interest in playing as well as listening to pop music, and feel his life is moderately satisfactory.

One British journalist, after describing such a young man, finished by writing:

> Yes, you could say that Nick was a layabout, and in the clinking and the smoke and the laughing, the coffee bar holds many like

Joining together in adulation—one way of 'belonging'.

> him. Coffee bars, of course, exist even in the smallest towns of the land, and must collectively contain quite a few Nicks. There seem to be just two queries to utter: is the 'unemployed' really a bigger group than 'they' say it is; and is there any possibility that being 'unemployed' may be a good career?

Some observers feel that the rise in unemployment has also been an inducement for young women to bear and rear babies—whether or not the baby's father marries them. With State support, local authority housing and more liberal attitudes to such things, it is a kind of career—though like other marginal solutions it entails long-term strains.

Identity outside work

Our impression is that the potential for turning the misfortune of involuntary unemployment to constructive purpose depends on resourcefulness in the development of interests. Young people who react by taking to their beds and mooning around the house all day are not showing resourcefulness. Restless activity of an indiscriminate kind, filling time with TV, comics, hanging about on the streets or watching football is little better.

Of course the best solution is to assure the possibility of employment, but when that is not immediately possible, the issue is how the young unemployed can develop life-enhancing interests. Options include undertaking some sort of community service, further education such as evening classes, or forming groups with alternative values outside straight society. In this way they may acquire a new identity—as Nick shows signs of doing—which is not dependent on the status offered by paid work and may be redeployable in new activities and interests in later life.

This is a promising and constructive response to being unemployed, but it is not easy or possible for everyone. And since being unemployed in modern society is something for which people are often not to blame, we believe that society owes more to the unemployed than barely enough money not to go hungry. In the age of the silicon chip, the number of people unemployed through no fault of their own is going to increase. The effort to help them to develop resourcefulness and find enough interests to feel that their lives are not wasted will require a massive community effort. This is a matter of enlightened self-interest as well as altruism. Sooner or later, we who are in work may be of their number.

Alternative living

A story is told of a meeting some years ago between one of the leading figures of the London 'underground' and an old friend who was insensitive enough to ask him what work he was doing. In magisterially contemptuous tones came the reply: 'I don't work, I play.' Richard Neville, describing the hippies of the

1960s, considered this to be the essence of their attitude to life and society. 'Dropouts are anticipating future economic policy,' he wrote in 1970. Fred Davis found the same of the hippies in San Francisco's Haight-Ashbury.[8] Others have echoed this theme: 'We are secret agents of a future society free from the routine degradation of work,' in the words of the leader of the London Street Commune, and 'Tomorrow you may be paid not to work—can you take it?' asks Richard Mills[9] in *Young Outsiders in London.*

One way to adapt to unemployment is by a pre-emptive strike—you 'drop out'. However, many people who drop out do so not because they cannot find work, or fear that they will not be able to, but because they wish to avoid the sorts of job which are available to them. Others actively seek a quite different style of life.

Brave new world?

Fred Davis points out that in the USA dropping out has become an essentially middle class revolt against the consumer society from which the young people benefited as children. They could, in many cases, find a rewarding place in that culture but choose to drop out in favour of what they regard as a more genuine lifestyle. Many of those who were drawn to the Haight-Ashbury district in the flower power era of the 1960s were fleeing from homes unsettled by their parents' own conflicts over the cultural values of the acquisitive society. Others simply wanted to be where the action was.

Although dropping out is beginning to be more common in middle life, most thorough-going dropouts are young adults. They reject conventional family life, excess material possessions, competitiveness and the traditional work ethic in favour of doing full-time what they value most—living for *now*, or living 'naturally', or living responsibly (ecologically). They may study or engage in art, crafts, writing, politics, child-rearing, sex, or exploration of the mind (whether through drugs, meditation or religion). Some try to implement their values politically, as with the Ecology Party, now established in France and Britain.

'Work' takes on new meanings

All these occupations are, of course, recognisable to the straight world they wish to leave behind. The difference is that if you are a dropout, you do not look for a job in the straight world. You live off the State or your family, or you make do with what you can earn at casual jobs. You do not expect to have a career but only to find immediately meaningful occupations for yourself. There is a range here of egocentric motives and pursuits, at one extreme, and altruistic ones at the other. Some mystical or crypto-religious groups combine the two. Some male dropouts send their girlfriends out to earn money as secretaries and receptionists in the straight world.

Personal relationships are seen as much more important than activities or possessions. A nine-to-five job would be unthinkable, although it must be emphasised that many dropouts work very hard—in their own time and on activities of their own choosing. The work they do is inextricably linked to fun, drugs, music, and communal living. There is often a strong element of defiance of authority, and a lack of class consciousness, though others are militantly political, espousing Marxist or other radical ideals.

Groups of like-minded people

Though there are still hermits, most of those practising an alternative lifestyle exist in communities or cult groups. It is easier to go against the customs of one's family and society in the company of others of like mind. Young people deviating together can offer each other comfort or approval, and employ boundary-maintaining actions to ward off the outside world; they may eat only health foods, grow beards or long hair, wear demins and T-shirts all the time and everywhere (just as much a boundary-maintaining uniform as the three-piece pinstripe suit).

Distinctive 'uniforms' or paraphernalia give a small group a sense of cohesiveness by setting it apart from 'the rest of them'.

Alternative communities vary greatly in size, stability and homogeneity, and contain individuals who are there for many different reasons.[10] Some groups have a definite purpose, ideology or philosophy, while others share the same accommodation more or less by chance. There is a wide range of living arrangements. They may be urban or rural, organised round a charismatic leader or not, may or may not experiment with group sex and group child-rearing, may or may not attempt to produce their own goods or be self-sufficient, and so on. The central common theme is the attempt by young adults to form alternative ways of living, different from established patterns.

Many communities and communes eventually break up, and many individuals, either from choice or necessity (as after an illness, hunger, or a bad experience), retreat back to the straight world. But the alternative society phenomenon in its various manifestations remains immensely important because it offers the chance of self-esteem and the development of many interests to young people who for one reason or another do not fit into or do not like the ordinary world. It also stimulates changes in the 'straight' world. These alternative society types have shown our generation how it may be possible to consider other values and interests, potentially enriching our own working life, and life generally. They may be less equipped to achieve their own aims than the people whose lifestyle they have condemned (the movement has not been going long enough for us to know how well such people face the challenges of later stages of life). But they have raised the awareness of the rest of us to many important issues, upset the complacent and persuaded many others to take a fresh look at their lives and possibly get out of a rut.

An international network

The pattern we have been describing is that of children of the 60s. Other alternative society groups are different in their values, clothing, language and behaviour. The 1960s people emphasised love and peace. 'Make love, not war' they chanted in their revulsion against Vietnam. Even the notorious Family of Charles Manson, the commune of young Californians whose horrifying history shocked the world in the early 1970s, claimed that they had committed their revolting crimes in the name of love. But sex and anti-war protests were only part of the picture. One of the most striking features of the phenomenon has been that it has formed an international network.

The alternative youth culture is international, cutting across national boundaries and drawing its adherents together by appealing to universal aims.

Unlike the earlier colony-like bohemias—the Latin Quarter of Paris, London's Bloomsbury and New York's Greenwich Village—modern youth culture has spread throughout Western society, and enabled young people of many countries to move around inside that culture, visiting, gossiping, reading poems, passing on drugs, exchanging political ideas. The values of instant generosity, sharing and hospitality are practised.

Don't just sit there . . .

This new culture has sought to forge a better relationship between ideals and behaviour, emphasising *doing*, rather than just passively watching other people do. They do not just go to concerts, they make their own music—often to a high standard. They do not merely read poetry, but write it. They do not merely bewail the plastic food of the supermarket, but insist on natural products, and when they can they grow their own. They do not merely attack the impersonality of modern life, but try to do something about it—by creating their own sub-cultures, or a new pattern of work based in the home. They write and publish their own newspapers. All this is seen as an attempt to assume responsibility for important aspects of living, instead of leaving them to professionals or specialists. For everyone is regarded as having the capacity to express himself creatively and take care of his own needs.

Dropouts as others see them

Many older people secretly admire these young adults' lifestyles—and particularly their courage in protesting against racism and bloodshed and allowing freer scope for their sexual and other feelings. Sometimes older people have tried to join in, at least in part or for a short time. Some of the encounter groups which have sprung up in the last few years, or the straw-hut holidays made popular by Club Méditerranée, are attempts to give the middle-aged a chance to feel that they, too, can get rid of their formalities and inhibitions (though many young people may regard these efforts, perhaps rightly, as pathetic).

However, young people of this type also arouse hostility. They are distrusted as irresponsible, feared as unhealthy (for example in spreading venereal disease, pushing drugs, or living in insanitary conditions), and disliked for their hypocrisy (for example in begging money from those whom they despise for earning it). Alternative society, like straight society, has its black sheep. At best, officialdom tends to make dropouts' lives difficult. In Britain, for instance, which treats them by and large with benign tolerance, the authorities pursue a policy of minor harassment. In some areas they have come to terms with squatting, so at least these impoverished young people normally have somewhere to live, but they are constantly being 'moved on'. When the young started sleeping out in parks, the parks were closed, and so on. Whenever one drug is being abused, stocks are destroyed or regulations tightened up, which has led to another drug filling its place. (This was one cause of the dramatic recent rise in heroin addiction in Britain.)

Misfits or pioneers?

Not only do outsiders react in different ways to the alternative society; so do the young people who enter it. Many of them live up to its ideals; many do not, and use it as a way of justifying a life of petty crime. Some are attracted to it in the first place because of their own inadequacies. Richard Mills had this to say of London's alternative youth society:

> Among the groups in which I moved, it was never wholly clear who were the ones who would be able to get by in conventional society and who were those, so bereft of the skills (conventional society) requires, (who) would be destitute outsiders all their days, but that there are many of the latter was quite clear.

It is still too early for us to know how well young people of this kind in the 1970s will adapt to middle and old age in the 1980s and 1990s. But plenty of them have already dropped back into more conventional ways of living because they disliked one or more aspects—for instance, the intense jealousy they felt when they were expected to share sexual partners (even if they disapproved in theory of the possessiveness of monogamy), or the sheer physical discomfort. Or perhaps they just grew into the next stage of life, which emphasises commitment to a more productive set of values.

It looks as if these alternative ways of living are what psychologists call 'temporary communities', providing a 'transitional learning experience'. Mills believes that society should treat such groups with 'benign neglect'. We ourselves believe that they should be actively welcomed, for they can encourage spontaneity, flexibility and the development of resourcefulness and offer the opportunity to develop interests, which is difficult to do within the constraints of a straight job, and they may stand many individuals in good stead all through life. And, just as important, they offer a chance of some happiness, self-esteem and personal development to many young people who may feel themselves to be misfits, perhaps justifiably discouraged at their prospects in the ordinary institutions of society.

5 Establishment

Conventionally, though not for the people going through them, earlier phases of the life cycle are rather like rehearsals—young people explore, prepare, practise and play with ideas, relationships, jobs and leisure interests. These experiences prepare them for the 'main act' of their lives, which comes with what we have called the establishment phase. This phase—the prime of life, full adulthood, the productive years—constitutes a keystone of our lives: in advanced countries it lasts, very approximately, from the ages of 25 to 55. We call it the establishment phase.

Investing in life

Suppleness of mind is as important as suppleness of body.

In a sense, 'rehearsing' goes on throughout life; but during the establishment phase most people settle on certain relationships, ideas and activities to commit themselves to and spend their energies on. During these years, however various their styles of life, most people's main preoccupation is with what we would call *major life investments*—work, family, friends, community activities, and values. Obviously we use the word investment not merely to cover financial commitments like mortgages, but to cover personal involvements; for people invest bits of themselves, as well as what they earn, in the pattern of life they adopt. And that is true whether they have chosen their lifestyle, inherited it or had it thrust upon them.

Traditional patterns

Typically, in advanced societies nine out of ten adults get married, and during the establishment phase most couples have two or three children. (Many couples have much larger families; others have no children, some by choice, others involuntarily. We do not exclude the latter or treat them as 'deviant'.) When those who are parents near the end of the phase, their children generally leave the parental home as they enter work or further education, eventually establishing homes of their own.

The phase traditionally applied to this period is 'getting married and living happily ever after'. The husband is the breadwinner, securely employed in a job that brings him ever greater rewards until he retires; his wife is his helpmeet, a devoted homemaker and mother whose outside interests do not interfere with her basic job as housewife, child-bearer and child-

Digging in, settling down—a component of a day's fun, and also a rehearsal for long-term commitment.

rearer. Many people will recognise this model as the ideal presented to them as they were growing up, and it remains, as we have seen, the lifestyle which many young people still either aspire to or expect. But now it is merely one among many possible models, for several changes are altering the traditional picture.

A changing world

People live longer and society is changing more rapidly. As a consequence, the expectation that things will remain stable for 30 years is less warranted than in the past. People are more likely to change their jobs, their employers, even their occupations, one or more times during their active lives. One of the by-products of technological advances in medicine is birth control. Women can plan their pattern of fertility in a way that was previously impossible, and they and their offspring are likely to survive childbirth more than ever before. Young people marry earlier than previously, can plan to have fewer children in a shorter space of time, and wives are freed to return to the job market in early middle life. This leaves them with up to 20 years of employment ahead of them, even after having left the world of work for a time when children arrived.

The job a wife and mother returns to may well be quite different from the job she had before marriage. With a longer life ahead of her, it is not necessarily disastrous, because the earlier choice may not have been right in the long term. And while the struggle to open new opportunities for women continues, there is a need in each individual's life to cope with what is available 'here and now'. Cross-switching careers, whether because of inner boredom or change of external circumstances, requires flexible adaptation to new life circumstances. We believe that having this capacity, or developing it as the need arises, helps people to grow.

Society on the move

A change of scene, a change of pace, is stimulating. It prevents us getting bored and can help us to survive in an uncertain and changing world. After all, 40 or more years in the same job can get very dull. And where boredom is not recognised and dealt with—for instance by job enrichment, sabbatical leave, switching jobs inside an organisation—there can be trouble. Both in Britain and the USA observers have suggested that some unofficial strikes are caused by the desire for excitement and drama in lives that are spent on dull, repetitive work.

In situations of rapid change people are required to move around if they wish to maximise their economic opportunities. Big industries require their key staff to move from posting to posting, and career advancement is often tied to being responsive to opportunities to move. As the computer age makes more and more jobs and even whole industries obsolete, more working people have to move on to find new jobs if they wish to remain gainfully employed at all. The movement from the country to the towns which began in the Industrial Revolution has been given another boost by the mechanisation of farming. And more than ever before, opportunities for developing and expressing leisure interests have now become concentrated in towns.

Many people have no choice about moving: they are forced to move to make way for housing developments or motorways, and their houses may be bought under a compulsory purchase order. In Britain, the immense building programmes of the years following the Second World War meant that many working class people were rehoused—often miles away from their original local neighbourhoods, which provided 'natural' bonds for informal recreation and leisure activities.

The well-off, too, are frequently on the move. Everywhere, second homes have become more common, whether it is a mobile home or a cottage, whether it is in Wales or the Dordogne, in Martha's Vineyard or on Lake Tahoe. The typical British second-home owners are a couple in their thirties with two children under 14. They use the second home for holidays and weekends, and may plan to retire to it eventually. In Britain, more perhaps than in America, it may provide a source of informal extra income through holiday lettings, at a stage of life when family expenses are high.

Divorce and after

So, though this is the most stable phase of life, change and movement are more frequent than one would suppose. Families change homes, schools, jobs, cars and sometimes spouses in the course of this period. Divorce and remarriage are now common in this part of the life cycle. Between 1961 and 1970 the number of second marriages in which both parties had been married before increased in Britain from 21,000 to 32,000; second marriages in which only one partner had been married before rose from 36,000 to 49,000. In the old days, when life expectancy for both sexes was much shorter and maternal mortality was much higher, few marriages lasted longer than 20 years. A 25-year-old couple marrying in Britain today can expect to live another half century. But will they spend the whole of that time together? Current estimates are that about 40 per cent of marriages contracted today will end in divorce.

Some people feel that the best way to protect ourselves from the traumatic consequences of divorce, given its increased probability, is to lower our expectations of marriage, because with idealisation comes disillusionment. Others disagree, because without ideals there is no joy of fulfilment. Our view is that the dilemma can be side-stepped by concentrating on equipping ourselves, and re-equipping ourselves at each stage, with interests which can be employed to facilitate growth and adaptation as challenging situations arise. It is the rigidity of the ideals rather than idealism itself that brings marriages to grief.

Attitudes to affluence

But what kinds of interest might they be? Money helps, but it does not provide all the answers. People are much better off financially than they used to be—all those telephones, hi-fis, gadget-packed homes, second cars, second homes, even second

The stereotype . . .

wives bear witness to the fact. Yet there is a negative reaction to affluence as well as an enjoyment response, and many dissidents and proponents of alternative lifestyles emphasise healthier and more natural-oriented values and less consumerism. Many people wonder whether overtime and overwork are really worth it. Do we pay too high a price for purely material rewards?

Shifting sex roles

Along with these changes in material values, one of the most significant changes in Western society since the Second World War has been the change in sex roles—and the change in awareness of them. Feminism has been with us as a significant social movement since Mary Wollstonecraft and Abigail Adams, but apart from a few isolated success stories, the steam appeared to go out of the women's movement of the early 20th century. Women paused at their interim success in obtaining the franchise to vote, and accepted the conventional division of labour at home for another half century. The norm was for men to go out to work at a workplace which was stereotyped as 'masculine' (tough, active, competitive and ambitious), while women stayed at home, which was stereotyped as 'feminine' (loving, supportive, passive and non-competitive).

Not any longer. This is not the place to analyse why women have risen up in their millions and demanded equal pay and equal opportunity, and why equal pay and opportunity laws have been passed; suffice it to say that women increasingly see themselves as legitimately having a work life as well as a domestic life, like men. The proportion of married women who earn

And the evolution of a new set of values for women.

money outside the home has more than doubled in Britain over the past 25 years, rising from 22 per cent in 1951 to 49 per cent in 1976. They now form, in Britain, 25 per cent of the workforce, and in the US 40 per cent.

Options for women

Women may work continuously, or drop out when they have children, or stop briefly while their children are young. They may work because of economic pressures—either because they are single, with or without children, or because their husbands are not highly paid. Or they may wish to keep their marketable skills employed in case they lose their husbands, now that divorce is so much more common. Or they may work because they are better educated and have been brought up to seek the same self-expression through employment as men; or they may emphasise the extent to which they enjoy the stimulation and interest of having a job, working outside the home with others, and being paid for it. Even if their husbands are well paid and they do not 'need' to work for financial reasons, they often nowadays choose to do so—which is a significant indicator of women's new determination to work at something besides being good wives and mothers. Among those who are poorly paid, or in jobs which are dull, many naturally feel 'alienated' from their occupations, as would men in the same circumstances; but the majority of women now feel that they have a part to play in the world beyond the four walls of home, and that work has a part to play in their personal and family lives. The issues have centred on how to manage it—and this has required special resourcefulness.

Fathering has become a neglected role in our society—with more mothers going out to work fathers may come into their own again.

A new focus for men

Many men's attitudes are changing, both towards their own work and towards their family life.[1] In some cases they are taking more part in domestic duties—from giving the occasional helping hand to willingly taking their full share of organising the household and looking after the children. One reaction to the feeling of meaninglessness they may experience in factories and offices, and the demands made on their private life by overtime, has been to enrich their private lives, often in the home. Many have placed their own ceiling on career advancement if it means they will constantly be away from home, or working overtime in the evening or at weekends.

Not all men who de-emphasise the Protestant work ethic automatically become family men or supporters of the women's cause. Many seek private gratification through leisure activities, and there is now much more stress on the kind of lifestyle made possible by certain jobs. One South Coast English firm of solicitors, for example, advertised for an associate who 'likes to potter around with boats'. American universities which are near ski resorts or in warm climates find it easier to attract staff. Many firms now make a point of mentioning attractions which have stricly speaking nothing to do with the jobs for which they are recruiting.

More choice all round

Because of all these changes the establishment phase is a good deal less static and predictable than it used to be. The choices available to or thrust upon individuals are much more numerous. A man may work, and not his wife (the conventional pattern), they may both work continuously (the dual-worker pattern), or they may work alternately or part-time (the work-sharing pattern). They may work as a partnership or separately.

It has always been fairly common in the United States for a young wife to work to finance her husband through college, even through prolonged studies like medicine or law. Now a young wife frequently has her children while her husband establishes himself, then finishes a training while her husband supports her. He, in turn, may go on to further training or simply take time out in later years while she earns the family living. Increasingly, a woman's earnings are accepted as part of the family economic resources, for instance in mortgage applications. Yet ten years ago this was almost impossible in Britain.

Erik Gronseth,[2] the Norwegian sociologist, has been doing research into new patterns of 'work-sharing' in families. In Norway and elsewhere employers are experimenting with flexible work hours ('flexi-time') and a shorter working week, which are likely to become more and more acceptable as the numbers of unemployed rise. Some workers may use the 30-hour or four-day week as an opportunity to take on a second job, 'moonlighting' to earn extra tax-free money to keep pace with inflation or raise the family's standard of living. Their wives may then have an even greater burden of housework than before. But in theory the shorter and more flexible working week gives both sexes more time to devote to other interests, including their families and friends.

The family life cycle

We divide the establishment period not into decades, or into age categories, but into sub-phases which are marked by different stages of the family cycle. For families with children the family cycle is punctuated by events in the lives of parents and children which affect the whole domestic unit; for childless families similar preoccupations prevail but take different forms.

Sub-phase	Preoccupation	Potential problems
Early establishment (pre-school children)	Concern with *productivity*: choices and plans	Conflicts in the allocation of one's energies
Mid-establishment (children at school)	Concern with *performance*: effectiveness; competence at what is chosen	Conflicts of loyalties and obligations; dissatisfaction
Late establishment (children out of school)	Concern with *evaluation*: the meaningfulness of commitments (psychological 'payoffs')	Depression, boredom; feelings of being trapped, isolation; whether to change (what? how?)

Naturally, few family life cycles fit perfectly into this pattern, but our table offers a rough guide to the major preoccupations and the likely problems of most parents while they have children at home. Individuals still have some of their previous preoccupations, but they are likely to be of less central concern. Similarly, people who postpone parenthood or have their children very young, or have a partner much older or younger than themselves, will have a different experience of the sub-phases. There are biological elements in the experience, as well as psychological ones, so age does play a part. But by and large the main differences stem from how people deal with these preoccupations.

Transitions smooth or troubled

Some people make the transitions comparatively easily, experiencing relatively little tension in dealing with the problems, they present. Others find them so disturbing that they begin to doubt themselves and their major life choices. They may feel that it was a mistake to marry, or to have married their particular spouse, or to have tied themselves into a particular career. This is the 'mid-life crisis', which acts like a dormant volcano during this phase. Disturbed by the doubts and recriminations that well up inside them, some people may opt out of one of the things to which they have committed themselves in the young adult stage—their work, their marriage, or a major sphere of interest. Others hold out, seeking a resolution of their problems. If this does not come, they may opt out at a later stage.

The degree of anxiety and concern experienced depends on a great many factors: biological and psychological make-up, hormonal changes associated with ageing, the way previous dilemmas were resolved, and also on things in the environment like public opinion, the immediate network of relationships and opportunities for redeploying one's activities.

Early establishment phase

The main preoccupation of adults at this stage of their lives is with *productivity*. By productivity we do not only mean earning enough money to house, feed and clothe the family; we mean also all those activities, interests and associations which contribute to the wellbeing of the family and the flourishing of people's lives in the community around them. Home-making, looking after the children, keeping one's marriage in good repair and getting on with parents and in-laws and other relatives all need to be worked at, just as does a paid job. The work is psychological and social work, necessary to the kind of growth we are considering.

Early establishment—time to start applying the lessons learnt in earlier phases.

Productivity means survival

Human beings are concerned with productivity in this broad sense at most stages of their lives, but it is in the early establishment phase that it preoccupies them most, partly

because they are at a point in their life cycle at which they will have established a personal identity, chosen an intimate life partner, and will be required by the nature of life in our society to be productive if they are to survive. These are economic pressures to establish a home and family life, and many young parents feel caught in what sociologist Harold Wilensky calls a 'life-cycle squeeze'.

The central problem, given the limitations of time, is how to *allocate their energies.* Many people feel there is not enough time in the day, and that they do not have the strength to fit in everything they need or would like to do. They are constantly faced with difficult choices. For example, a wife might like to take an extra qualification but feels that she cannot do that and have a baby, which she also wants, particularly if she is expected to back up her husband. A husband might like to be with his family but have to be available on his job if he is to advance in his career, which he must do if he is to meet his family's increasing financial needs. And what about fitting all these in with his ambition to stand for election to his local council or trade union? It is a period when money is usually tight, as the family's needs for housing, furnishing, baby things and so on are growing faster than earnings.

Research on families shows this general picture, but it is important to remember how varied people's solutions to these problems are: some people spend a little energy on a great many different things, others concentrate their energy on one or two areas of life to the virtual exclusion of everything else. Location, social class, availability of opportunities, personal temperament and marital relationship obviously all make a difference.

The conventional family

There are several patterns, the most culturally supported of which is what we call the conventional pattern. This pattern has been dominant in all classes in the Western world since the Industrial Revolution, when new wealth eventually freed millions of women from the need to work. (Even now, many newly prosperous working class families regard a non-working wife as a status symbol—and of course many wives are pleased to give up a job which is little more than low-paid drudgery.)

This conventional model has been very well described for the Canadian suburban family by the American sociologist David Riesman:

> The husbands work all day in the city; they pride themselves on being practical no-nonsense men—a pride partly maintained by polarising themselves from their allegedly emotional starry-eyed wives. The wives have the leisure and education and energy to make a career out of suburbia, and to be anxious about themselves and their children.[3]

Breadwinning for him . . .

In this pattern young husbands are expected to put most of their energy into their work. The lion's share of what they earn will probably be devoted to their homes and families. Conventional housewives do not work, and the income they formerly brought in will no longer feed into the family economy. If they are at the stage of moving from rented accommodation or the in-laws' home to a home of their own, there will be a deposit to put down, mortgage instalments to pay and consumer durables like washing machines and refrigerators to buy, quite apart from a car, telephone and other such goods if they expect to live at a high standard. If they are already in a home of their own, the husband's spare time is likely to be taken up with do-it-yourself improvements because there is too little money to employ carpenters and decorators.

For most people of course, home is not merely a shelter, but a social centre for the enjoyment of friendship and fun in privacy and comfort. It is also a place to keep and to display valued objects and possessions (family photographs, souvenirs, books, china ornaments), a way of presenting one's tastes and experience to those who enter it. With increasing affluence, these middle class values are spreading through the population, but of course there are many people whose income is too low to afford this standard of life, however much they might like it.

. . . and home-making for her

Mother and child alone together all day—the bliss of motherhood, or the trap of togetherness.

For conventional wives and mothers the main channel for expressing a preoccupation with productivity is home and family. The conventional wife who enjoys home-making and feels she has chosen the right husband may well be fully satisfied by this set of outlets for her productive energies. Cooking, shopping, visiting friends and the hairdresser easily fill the day. If she enjoys looking after children this may be the happiest time of her life. If she has a daily help or an au pair girl or there is a nearby day nursery which her children can attend, she will have more leisure than wives in other kinds of marriage, and she may be able to keep up with her old interests or form new ones.

The price to be paid

The problems that this type of marriage holds for many wives only become apparent at a later stage. After a while she may, now that so many mothers work outside the home, feel secretly guilty that she has no plans to do so. But today's conventional husbands, putting nearly all their energies into work, also face a real conflict.

Most men are no longer content to leave bringing up the children entirely to their wives. They want to see something of them and play a real role in their lives. And most wives, even conventional ones, now want their husbands to share in this task, and expect them to share the chores as well. The husband may experience considerable strain in trying to meet all of his wants and his wife's expectations as well, and quarrels may ensue. Young children may suffer, too, scarcely seeing their father and having a mother who is irritable and resentful, perhaps feeling trapped in her chosen conventional role. If one or the other of the parents does have time to pursue outside interests, he or she may do so increasingly without the partner (because of the difficulty of finding baby-sitters); this, too, may lead to problems.

Interests are more likely to be shared and centred around the home. But activities like decorating and watching television offer limited scope for development. Betty Friedan describes vividly in *The Feminine Mystique* how a feeling of frustration builds up at the failure of even the most comfortable home to fulfil all the needs of the lively and educated woman.[4]

The captive housewife

If a woman accepts the conventional pattern but is less maternal, or is unhappily married, or has given up outside work that meant a lot to her, she may be thoroughly unhappy and frustrated. The conventional pattern may not be the right one. The British sociologist Hannah Gavron coined the phrase 'captive wife' to describe women in this situation.[5]

A captive housewife, stuck into a pattern that does not allow expression for her preoccupations, may try to find some outside interest to pursue, but in some circumstances, or with an unhelpful husband, it may be too difficult. This may be the unhappiest time of her life, when she feels it could be the happiest. Something has gone wrong. She has not been able to grow satisfactorily in this phase.

More about sex differences

Growth in the establishment phase depends on being able to develop interests which fit both spouses' preoccupations with productivity, and the options open to them. In our study of a sample of British husbands and wives who were university graduates, we compared their leisure activities in the establishment phase with those they pursued at university. Our results confirm that both sexes' interests become much more home-centred, that certain interests which were once very important to them are virtually given up. While that is true overall for men and women, there are some striking differences between the sexes, influenced by a mixture of personal inclinations, social norms and available resources.

On marriage, both sexes show a drop in their enjoyment of friends of the opposite sex. Both daydream less than they did, and no longer listen so much to music on their own. But while husbands' serious reading is still increasing, wives' serious reading drops dramatically. And while husbands enjoy visiting their relatives no more than they did when they were at university, and much less than they did when they were small children, wives enjoy seeing their families or in-laws twice as much as when they were children, and four times as much as when they were still at university. This confirms what has already been reported by researchers of working class families: that women mostly perform the function of linking the couple and their children with other relatives. It is also clear that women see

'Who said a quiet gossip?'—maybe not, but still an important social outlet for the housebound mother.

much less of their friends of the opposite sex than do their husbands, who may still have such contacts at work. And men continue to pursue leisure interests in pubs, clubs and sports grounds. Women have many fewer such outlets, and their continuation of independent activities on these lines while their husbands are at work is less approved.

But the older conventional pattern is giving way statistically to another pattern, which we have called the new conventional pattern.

The new conventionals

The new conventional family is one in which the husband's role is similar to that of the conventional husband, and in which his wife accepts that her *primary* role is as home-maker. But while she temporarily leaves her job to concentrate on home and children, she has every intention of returning to work when the children are 'old enough'. (How old is old enough varies from family to family.)

Her career remains important

Although in the early establishment phase there is no manifest difference between conventional and new conventional families, the very fact that the wife regards her future work as important makes an immense difference, both in practical and psychological terms. For one thing, the husband may willingly take a larger share of the domestic chores, to make it easier for his wife to prepare to return to work. For another, the wife may use any spare time to keep up with her former work—reading journals, going to meetings, keeping in touch with colleagues, perhaps taking a course. If her field of work is similar to her husband's, opportunities for keeping abreast are greater. If it is quite different, she still has something outside the home to talk about with her husband; her interests are not confined to domestic matters.

Whether such a wife goes back to work soon or delays her return will depend on various factors. For instance, she may enjoy domestic life more than she expected and find that she really wants to remain at home, perhaps having more children than anticipated. Then she may find herself a grandparent, and continue with domestic interests. If she finds she enjoys domesticity less, she may get back to work as soon as she can.

A woman may be unable to take a job because her husband is unhelpful and it is difficult to find a crèche, babyminder or mother's help and she has no relatives nearby who can help out. Or perhaps she needs the flexibility of part-time work but the only jobs available are full-time. If she is keen to get back to work but cannot find sufficient opportunities and supports, she may experience a good deal of frustration and resentment. She is stuck in the classic 'captive wife' position and may become depressed, or find herself increasingly at odds with her husband.

Returning to work

Returning to work is not simple. If a wife goes back after only a brief interlude at home she may have few difficulties. If her job is a good one, she will probably receive enough psychological and other rewards to counterbalance the extra load on both partners. (There will be an extra load, however good the arrangements for looking after the children are.) There is more money, each has a work interest, and the loss of other valuable interests because there is no time for them does not, perhaps, seem as important.

On the other hand, there are undoubtedly tensions which stem from the wife's re-entry to work and, if severe, they may threaten the relationship. These tensions will be made worse if the husband did not really want his wife to go back to work (or does not like the results), if there is too little time to fit everything in comfortably, if husband and older children feel neglected or overburdened with extra duties, or if family and in-laws (or friends and neighbours) disapprove rather than give support. And if things go wrong, she may have to face other people saying 'I told you so.'

The woman who has to return to work for financial reasons—her husband has an accident, or there is a bankruptcy, unemployment or illness—faces all these tensions but has the psychological advantage that she feels she has no choice in the matter. No one, not even her own conscience, can accuse her of being selfish and neglecting her family's interests. She is not betrayed from within.

Women who return after a prolonged absence also face special challenges which we shall take up in the next chapter.

The dual-worker family

The dual-worker family is one in which both wife and husband work continuously in paid occupation as well as having a family.[6] Countries vary in the amount of maternity leave that a woman is legally entitled to, but at least in this respect goverments are beginning to make it easier for women to combine having a family with having a career. In some countries, like Sweden, parents are given a choice as to whether it is father or mother who takes 'parental leave'. But adequate alternative child care is another matter. Working couples provide care for their pre-school children in a variety or ways—through relatives, live-in help, professionally run playgroups or nursery schools, co-operative or neighbourhood groups, or crèches attached to the workplace. While there is strong support for universally available nursery schools for infants from the age of two or three, the issues of what kinds of school and how they are to be financed remain vexed.

Couples obviously vary in how committed each partner is to work and family roles, how full-time their work is, how equal they rate themselves, and how equally they actually share out the domestic work. Sometimes the wife works continuously but part-time; her job may be seen by both partners as less important than his. Both husband and wife may have jobs, though she is lower paid and effectively has two jobs, one at work, the other at home.

The symmetrical relationship

A more egalitarian couple, both with full-time jobs, will consider that each has the right to the same consideration as the other in all family decisions; for instance, they may decide to move to another town because the *wife* has been offered a much better job, or decide *not* to move even though the husband has the chance of a better job because there would be no chance of the wife finding the kind of work she would like in the new area.

This is what Michael Young and Peter Willmott have described in *The Symmetrical Family*—a family in which it is recognised that each partner has two jobs, one outside and one inside the home.[7] But it is very difficult to manage this kind of 'symmetry' unless the husband does far more at home than is usual, and it remains an 'ideal' towards which many families are striving rather than a widely prevalent pattern.

Special strains

The strains of a dual-worker pattern are considerable at present. The wife may be torn between home and work and feel she does justice to neither. She may resent turning over the baby to a helper and at the same time feel that she cannot give as much time or energy to her job as she would like. Or she may feel that her husband, in spite of his good intentions, is not doing his fair share of the domestic chores, and she can never relax and forget about child care or home maintenance in the same way that he can when he turns things over to her.

The husband may feel that he is helping out quite a lot but that his wife is not grateful enough. Or he may feel guilty if he sees that his wife is under strain yet he cannot do more to pull his weight at home. He may also feel that having to help so much in the house is hindering him in his career, that he is doing less than he is capable of, and that his friends consider him odd or do not include him in things he would like to do with them. None of this helps their relationship, unless they can talk it through honestly.

Special strengths

Yet, in spite of the dangers and difficulties, we found that, at least among the highly qualified British couples we talked to, those who had this kind of symmetrical relationship—both with careers, both sharing the responsibilities of home—actually enjoyed everyday activities as much or more than did conventional couples, dispelling the myth that this pattern necessarily erodes a marriage. Dual-worker marriages have special strains and vulnerabilities, but they have strengths as well. And conventional families also have both. While the risk of marital breakdown is at present higher with dual-worker families—partly because of lack of support—the picture of a conventional father saying goodbye to his conventional wife because she has not 'grown' over the years is also very familiar.

The key to enjoyment, and the marital satisfaction associated with it, is the capacity to grow into the new pattern, whichever it is—to find ways for both members to be productive in ways that fit their individual needs, rather than fitting willy-nilly into a predetermined formula.

Mid-establishment phase

By the time the children are all settled at school, their parents too are likely to be more settled: the husband has fixed on his career, the wife has adapted to whatever combination of domesticity and outside occupation she has chosen (or had wished upon her); they feel at home in their neighbourhood. Both have more idea than when they were younger of what they want to do, and of how to achieve it. And they have begun to learn the art of the feasible, and perhaps even more important the art of *accepting* the feasible, with all its limitations.

None of this necessarily means that they are settled in the sense of sitting back or grinding along in a groove. This is a kaleidoscopic phase in which they are likely to be busier than ever; more demands are made on them by their children and by the outside world. Every day brings new dramas, every year new teachers, new schools, new friends, new triumphs and tragedies. But with luck they are more relaxed about themselves, there is a bit more money to spare, and they have learned how to make way for the development of their own interests, as well as assuring that job, home and children survive.

More scope for enjoyment

This stage is potentially one of the most pleasurable. By now adults have provided for themselves some kind of working answer to that gnawing question of youth 'Who am I?', and after doing the necessary work of linking themselves in early adult life to the social institutions around them, they are ready to attend to personal interests. While people in this phase are not as physically active in sport as in their younger years, they put a lot of energy into other kinds of agreeable activities. This is the peak period not only for home-based hobbies like carpentry and gardening, but for family-centred activities like holidays and excursions into the country and visits to swimming pools, art galleries and zoos. Bringing up children is seen to be fun as well as a duty. Many people, as we have already noted, acquire a second home where they can relax and get back to nature. They may do some fishing or country walking; the children may go canoeing or pony-trekking. Other families may get a boat (one of the growth industries in Britain and America in the last 15 years) or take up camping as a leisure pursuit.

A chance to experiment

There is a general readiness at this stage to enjoy life, having made some pretty heavy investments in it. As an established couple you may try out new dishes and new places to eat. You may learn a bit about wine. You may try to improve your sex life, even going so far as to experiment with 'alternative' sex, have a discreet 'matinée' affair or subscribe to a specialist book or film club. You may try to renew your athletic prowess and take up jogging or competitive sport. Perhaps you will become adventurous again, and sail round the world or join mountaineering expeditions. There is even some evidence, perhaps more in America than in Britain, that taking part in some kind of psychiatric or 'experience' group, discussing your own and other people's problems is the intellectual equivalent of the working man's strikes—a way of taking time out of the grind of work and getting extra excitement. Encounter groups, Transcendental Meditation and other such experiential activities can serve this kind of purpose.

Financial comfort at last

All this experimentation depends, to a certain extent, on having a basic level of economic wellbeing, decent housing, good health and so on. Otherwise you are likely to have to concentrate on survival. But it also depends on your capacity to grow, to develop interests. Working class couples, many of whom have as high an income and perhaps even greater economic and housing security than middle class families, are often less enterprising about pursuing new interests (though any such generalisation is bound to have plenty of exceptions).

Again, balance is important. It is easy for the consumer interests of this phase to get out of hand. The individual who can never have enough consumer goods, and surrounds himself with hi-fis, cars, televisions and the like, may be storing up future trouble rather than developing resourcefulness by cultivating interests. People can become so obsessed with one activity, like

TV viewing, that they experience something like an addiction; or they can cast about so indiscriminately that they never get satisfaction from anything they try. All the same, if they do not have the chance to indulge themselves a bit at this stage there is a risk of getting into a rut, eventually suffering psychosomatic or depressive illness. They may come to feel that they are too stupid, useless, unattractive or incompetent to be able to get any pleasure out of life, and this is also an attitude which is antithetical to growth.

Always allowing for variations, research shows that the three main types of family which we described earlier tend to experience this mid-establishment phase in different ways.

The conventional wife: loss of self-esteem

In the *conventional family*, the particular danger is that once the children are away at school all day, and even more so later when they have left home, the wife will feel that she has lost part or all of her occupation. Of course she will still be occupied at home; the children will need feeding when they return from school, or ferrying to and from music classes or riding lessons. But there is a danger that, if she does not develop interests of her own, she will continue to be too protective towards her children when they are beginning to want and need some independence. Later on, she may find it hard gradually to loosen her control, allowing the children some private freedom away from her questions and concern.

This is the moment when some conventional wives begin to think of taking a job, coming into the 'new conventional' category. Unfortunately, we know that it is particularly difficult for many women to take up outside work again after several years confined to home-making. However good she was at her previous work, the typical conventional wife suffers a disproportionate loss of self-confidence when she tries to go back to it.

Even if she is still quite confident, the outside world does not make it easy for women to re-enter employment. There are too few possibilities for re-training, too few good part-time jobs (which are always much in demand) in a male-organised world. Her own psychological state and social factors may combine in a vicious circle. She may try less hard because she feels less likely to succeed, and she may decrease her chances of success because she does not put her best foot forward. And the disappointment and continuing feeling of uselessness may cause serious problems to her self-esteem and to her participation in family life.

Frustration can spell depression

We know from our own and others' research that her frustration may express itself in depressive illness. George Brown and Tirell Harris[8] have studied this in Britain, and Jessie Bernard[9] in America has conceptualised many of the issues, leading to the situation where captive wives, particularly those with few resources and an unsympathetic husband, suffer more illness, particularly mental illness such as clinical depression, than any other sub-group of the population. (The healthiest sub-groups are single, working women and young married men.) Brown and Bernard, as well as a number of 'male liberationists' like Warren Farrell, produce arguments and evidence in favour of the notion that a return to work benefits both husband and wife if they find themselves in this position of unsatisfying adaptation to the conventional mid-establishment pattern.

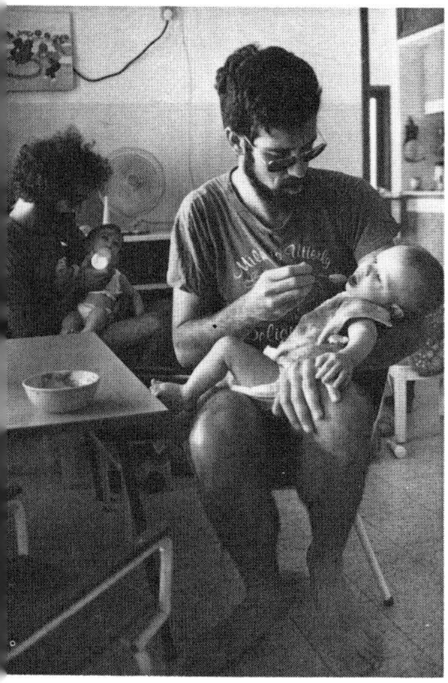

'I know I'm not as pretty as Mum, but eat it anyway!'

Stresses of the conventional husband

The conventional husband will probably have reached a fairly stable plateau in his career: he may be able to relax a little, and give more time to his family and other interests. But this is not always the case. The man who has a dull or exhausting job which he dislikes or finds boring may respond by taking to drink or gambling, or may sit around at home too tired or depressed to do much with or for his family or himself.

At the other extreme, men who are highly committed to their careers, perform successfully and are ambitious to reach the top are known from both British and American research to give much less time to their families. Such a husband may not be too happy about giving up his family and leisure interests, but may accept the change—and get his family to accept it—because of all the extra benefits promotion brings. He may feel that his wife is being given extra resources for the home and children. If she reckons this is not a fair exchange—more money for less interaction—quarrels are likely to erupt. And he may be laying up trouble with his children in the next stage of their lives. He may find that they hardly know him and feel that he has played little part in their upbringing—and tell him so.

When one partner grows faster another frequent problem in conventional families is a disparity in growth rates. The husband grows in confidence and develops psychologically through the challenges and wider experience offered by his work. His wife may be 'left behind', and both may feel acutely conscious of their growing differences. For some husbands and wives, it is not a crucial problem because neither needs to feel the 'equal' of the other; the disparity may suit them. For others it leads eventually to extra-marital affairs or divorce. Avoiding this kind of problem when the children are adolescent requires preventive action. Both parents need to find stimulating interests—other than child development for her and work for him.

The new conventional woman: anxieties . . .

The new conventional wife who always intended to return to work when her children were at school faces different problems from the conventional wife who never intended to work again but eventually decides to take a job out of desperation. As a new conventional wife she may have stayed in touch with her old firm or with any new developments in her field, and may have been talking about and planning her return for some time. So, although she may suffer from loss of confidence, it will probably be less severe. What she is more likely to suffer from, though, is cold feet. Will she be taking on too much? Will her boss be someone younger than she is? Will she really enjoy the nine-to-five atmosphere as much as she has enjoyed the comparative flexibility of domesticity? Will her husband help, not hinder? Will the children be OK? At a time when things are at a fairly 'stable' stage, she seems to be going back to the beginning. Is she strong enough, keen enough, young enough? She may be faced with a hard decision, especially if she suspects that her husband's encouraging remarks are only lip-service, or based on guilt.

Really determined wives will find a way, even in the face of opposition from their husbands. A national survey of British women showed in 1965 that one in six working mothers take jobs despite their husbands' objections.[10] However, those who are not determined enough to surmount all the obstacles may find it too difficult to return to work at all, despite all their intentions.

. . . myths . . .

Many wives deal with these difficulties, as the American sociologist Alice Rossi has indicated, by keeping a myth going in their minds that they will return perhaps to study for a higher degree—but later.[11] This kind of postponement Rossi likens to

> the romantic ideas of many people that they will one day write a great novel, although they do no writing apart from occasional correspondence to acquire the skills needed to write such a book. . . . In the process, they may be accumulating a considerable burden of unmet expectations with which they will enter middle age.

Hope deferred maketh the heart sick. Such a tactic stacks the odds against the realistic personal growth on which satisfaction depends. It is a very clear example of a problem which, if not properly solved at the time, is much harder to resolve later. 'Working through an acceptance of the probable limits of achievement they will reach in their lifetime', to quote Rossi, is a key task.

If a pattern of continuous postponement is likely to mean regrets and unhappiness in middle age, there are also immediate consequences for family relationships. Consciously or not, a woman may resent her husband (whose hostility or indifference may have been the last straw), and she may try to revitalise her life vicariously through her children. But if she never regarded her work as much more than a hobby, something that gave her an outside interest, giving it up may be a better solution for her than threatening the smooth running of her household and the comfort of the family. Many new conventional wives adopt an attitude of semi-commitment—telling others, and themselves, that they one day intend to take up their work again.

If a wife does successfully negotiate all the hurdles and return to work, the family has to adjust, both practically and psychologically. The extra income will no doubt be welcome, and it may be a particular delight to the wife that once again she is not dependent on her husband for all her spending money. (She may secretly have resented this, even if she accepted the conventional pattern.) But younger children may play her up, which can, of course, cause conflicts and doubt. Seeing other families which have adjusted successfully can be very encouraging at this point.

. . . and adjustments

The major cause of stress, however, is the reorganisation of domestic duties. It is often complicated in practical terms. It may be necessary to organise the family on a work-sharing system, or even to teach younger members how to prepare their own supper and how to work the washing machine, especially if there is no full-time help. So there is a great deal of training and reorganisation to be done, and unless it is done diplomatically (though firmly) a woman may find herself criticised for her bossiness.

A husband who has not had to prepare his own supper, sew on a button or cook a meal for five or ten years will not necessarily, overnight, be willing to undertake a larger share of the chores. If his wife is only working part-time, she may deal with the matter by doing all the work herself—the familiar 'Amazon' pattern. But if she is working full-time, and finds it tough going, it may prove very hard for her. Increasingly, women are trying to prepare for this by developing a more sharing pattern from the outset. But this may or may not be successful, and women are often their own worst enemies here as well as in the workplace. They feel so grateful for being loved that they accept domestic enslavement with relish. They are gratified if their husbands 'help a bit', 'give a hand with the washing up', 'do all the repairs and mend the fuses'.

Dual-worker families

Oddly enough, many dual-worker couples find the mid-establishment phase a bit easier than the earlier years of their marriage. This is partly because, since the wife has worked continuously from the beginning, her husband long ago became accustomed to it as a normal pattern. Ideally, he will have been drawn into doing a fairer share of the domestic chores and, now the children are at school, there is less to do. However, there will probably still be problems about looking after the children when school finishes, unless they have living-in help, special playgroup support or helpful relatives nearby.

Latch-key children

The great danger, particularly among less affluent or less resourceful families, is that their children will become 'latch-key kids' and take to watching television interminably. It is a matter of concern because indiscriminate viewing has an habituating effect, because unattended children face special risk and also because their energies are not being properly channelled and they are learning the negative lesson of being unresourceful.

Danger point

There is also a danger that both parents will become so interested and involved in their careers that they will be drawn in different directions, and feel eventually that they have grown apart (as with the conventional housewife and her husband). Many studies have shown that this period is psychologically a danger point for dual-worker families. However, if they survive this sticky patch, they have a strong plus in the unusually wide range of interests and experience that they will have developed. These provide resources for enjoyment with each other and with their growing children in years to come.

Late establishment phase

Once again, we can suggest only the most approximate ages for this phase of the normal adult's life cycle. We define it as the period when the children have left school and are beginning to leave home, so it can occur at any point in a 15-year span, from the parents' late thirties to their early fifties. But since people are marrying earlier and children are being born closer together, the late thirties and early forties are the more usual time. This phase also overlaps at the beginning with the mid-establishment phase, and at the end with the pre-retirement phase.

Taking stock

The main preoccupation now seems to be *revision.* In this stage one conducts a kind of interim personal audit of one's life. One begins to look back and wonder whether the commitments made in early adulthood to partners and jobs (or at least occupational lifestyle) have been the best one could have made.

The fortunate begin to say to themselves, 'I've not done too badly, all things considered', 'We've been pretty happy, on the whole', 'The children are turning out quite well', 'I wouldn't have chosen any other life', or 'I couldn't have had a better husband/wife.' They feel that there is a 'psychological pay-off' in terms of feeling happy and satisfied. Their life is rounding out and beginning to add up to a meaningful whole.

We must emphasise once again that all adults make some kind of revision continuously in their lives, but it does seem to become more of a preoccupation in this phase. It is also important to stress that one can feel 'happy and satisfied' even if (perhaps especially if) one has had setbacks and tragedies—for the satisfaction has a good deal to do with feeling that one has overcome the setbacks and survived the tragedies, that one's character has developed and one has the capacity to meet life's challenges with strength and resilience, long after one was supposed to have reached full maturity.

Responses to the awareness of death

At this stage people also begin to notice the decline in physical capacities which is a depressing feature of early middle age for nearly all or us. Sight, hearing, memory, the capacity to grasp and remember new information, stamina and strength all fade. People at this stage begin to be acutely, rather than vaguely, aware that they are not what they were and that they have a limited time to live. This is the period, as Elliott Jaques has

Indications of mortality can be a spur to make the most of what's left.

noted, in which death becomes more real in people's psychological lives.[12] There are many indications that the people who face this realisation best are those who have had, and still have, the capacity to explore and develop new interests. Many creative people have even found it to be a spur to new productivity. Those who do not may experience profound depression.

Others conclude from their 'revision' that they are unhappy and dissatisfied. Their characteristic feeling is restlessness. They may begin looking around to see if they might not do better with another kind of life, another kind of wife. They may simply experience an unaccountable malaise—'I know I have everything I want, but. . . .'

The children are leaving home, so if the parents remained together, consciously or unconsciously, 'for the sake of the children', they may now feel they have too little in common, and see no reason to remain together. There may be extra-marital affairs, and the proverbial 'empty nest' atmosphere may pervade the household. The wife may feel abandoned; the husband may feel ineffectual at home and throw himself deeper into his job or outside pursuits.

On the other hand, if the marriage was tense and stormy when the children were at home (a very common experience in families with adolescents), the atmosphere may suddenly become relaxed, a calm after the storm. Husband and wife have time for each other again, and they may use their new freedom to go out more, to develop new interests, or to travel together. Or they may use it to re-establish their sexual relationship. They no longer have to worry about the children walking in on them, or hearing what is going on, or calling out for attention.

At work too, there may be a feeling of anti-climax. One's

career has levelled off; one has reached one's ceiling, and the work is less demanding than it used to be. There are, of course, exceptions, like political careers or jobs in organisations which are very 'greedy' and absorbing. But most jobs require less of one, and one knows the limits of one's probable advancement.

Settling for the possible

To the extent that people begin to give up their former *unrealistic* hopes and dreams, they let up on driving themselves and as a consequence experience a better overall mental health. The psychological task now is to settle for what is possible, to give up ideas about what might have been but is now clearly impossible. This requires a kind of growth; if people hang on to their impossible dreams, they may become embittered and feel that what they are having to settle for is not good enough. If they are unable to face the realities of their situation, for whatever reason, they may feel very aggressive towards those they imagine have done them in. These feelings are sometimes displaced on to scapegoat figures, or, if no one else can be found to blame for one's dissatisfaction, turned back against oneself, only deepening the depression.

On the other hand, if they can confront the tasks of midlife and become what psychologist Daniel Levinson refers to as 'individuated', they are able to grow and enjoy some of the positive aspects of life in middle age.[13] If one sets one's ambitions at what one is likely to be able to achieve, one may well have the satisfaction of achieving them. A workman becomes foreman or shop steward; a manager gets a position on the board; a professional person is awarded an honour or is elected to office in a learned society. There is a pleasure in receiving recognition for one's achievements. But if someone is bitter about being blocked at shop steward level, or feels that the board should have made him chairman, or that the honours received were not enough—and he allows the disappointment to rankle—he will feel cheated at a time when he could feel gratified.

There are also pleasures in non-occupational life, where other interests may be developed and come to fruition. One may be gratified to see the results of one's efforts at helping younger people to develop their capacities in youth work, or at bringing about an improvement in local amenities, or at helping in an old persons' home, say by reading to the blind.

Fear of change

But research has shown that many middle-aged men are quite adept at building up defences against changing at this stage, either at work or in other spheres, fearing displacement by the new generation and redundancy as a result of technological innovations. To protect themselves against the real or imagined threat of a takeover by the young, they often become more rigid just at a time when they ought to be becoming more flexible if they are to grow adaptively.

Another way of meeting the challenge is by 'yielding' at work and putting more of one's energies into other interests, sometimes paid but often unpaid. Acting as secretary of the local sports club, judging at a local event like a flower show or county fair, being active in a charity—all of these activities offer respect and approval in a less demanding and competitive atmosphere.

Fear of success

At this stage some people face the problem of being far more successful than they ever dreamed. They may be surprised to find that success can bring its own problems. Matina Horner's point about women's fear of achievement in the male-dominated work world becomes salient again, for with career success, as with earlier stages, ambitious women must deal with the cultural equation of femininity with subservience.[14] With success they confront not only their own self-doubts, but the envy of others. For men, the problems of success stem from other sources. Freud attributed men's fear of success to fear of surpassing their father's level of achievement. The dread of retribution, rooted in the childish imagery of an overpowering father, can become a powerful force, even late in life. More recently, the Canadian organisational analyst L. J. Peter has noted a related phenomenon which he has dubbed the 'Peter principle', according to which organisations tend to push managers upward to the job *just above* their level of ability.[15] As this usually comes late in life, when abilities and ambition are moving in the opposite direction, the net effect may be disappointment—both for the organisation and for the individual.

There are often difficulties in middle age for people of modest background who do immensely well. Someone of working class background who does well at school and moves upward in the class scale by way of university has the advantage of developing a set of interests which can be shared with middle class neighbours and colleagues later on. But if they move up by way of business success only, buying their way into a middle class lifestyle without developing cultural interests to match, they may feel acutely that they do not fit into their new middle class circles. This can lead to considerable psychological difficulty. A husband may be embarrassed by his wife's behaviour or vice versa. The self-made man may develop social skill in the course of his success, but if his wife does not have the self-confidence and buoyancy to carry off social events, they may share less and less as years go on. He may seek another partner who will fit his new, more successful lifestyle.

Dealing with the menopause

For women, the late establishment phase coincides with the menopause. Its impact, even its physical symptoms, seem to be more marked for women who have not developed outside interests, hobbies or other occupations which give meaning and purpose to their lives once their children have left home.

One of the outlets for a woman's energies will still be her marriage, but there is a danger here of turning it into a substitute for the mother-child relationship recently lost. Much depends on diplomacy. She can, for example, encourage her husband to take exercise and keep fit—the forties are the dangerous age for coronaries—but unless she does it in a feeling of firm friendliness, she may be felt to be domineering or self-interested. (It may help if husband and wife are well matched physically, so that they can exercise together.) Above all at this stage, she can help him psychologically, if he has doubts and self-recriminations about what he has not achieved in life, by emphasising to him what he *has*.

Likewise, if she has no job of her own, now that she has time on her hands her husband can encourage her to develop new interests, perhaps by drawing her more into his work life. If he has a key job in his firm, or has been elected to public office, there will usually be a lot of out-of-hours entertaining or travel to which she can make a big contribution. Or he may help her to set up a business or take up a hobby or craft. And they may already have the joy of grandchildren, in whose lives they can play an immensely important part.

Work is therapeutic

But the best antidote to the conventional effects of the menopause seems to be a satisfying job. Many women who have been home-makers for 20 years or more and have never thought of returning to work now find that they want to. There are many encouraging examples of women who embark on public life or vocational training in their forties, and have the excitement of finding themselves useful and needed in another sphere. If a husband wants his wife's undivided attention at last, or wants to taper off activities or move to the country, he may be jealous of her renewal of interest in life. But, if the couple have a good relationship, they will be able to sort out their new pattern of conflicting interests and find a way for both to benefit from the wife's new vitality.

The energy and creativity that went into the family, can be re-directed in late midlife into more personal forms of expression.

The husband may find that helping her in her new interests is gratifying him at a time when he has achieved all he can in his own career. Whether or not he can be an active partner, he can start doing practical things for himself at home—like making his own lunch—which will free her to do what she wants to do. Even if she willingly stays at home to look after him, she may become resentful if he makes no move to enable her to develop interests now, after she contributed so much to give him support earlier. Issues of health, or worries about health, also begin to appear during this phase and may complicate the matter, affecting who is willing to do what to facilitate the other's development.

A new start for him and her

Many couples feel at this 'revision' stage that they have come out better than they expected as a couple. They feel they have done well with their family, in their work and in their social lives. This contributes to a feeling of great confidence, and they are likely to feel like tackling something completely new. The years that stretch ahead are seen as offering new opportunities, and the fact that there is likely to be more of them than in past times is seen as something to relish.

They may decide to do something they have always wanted to do and never had time for: this late sub-phase of the establishment period may inspire a deliberate effort to bring into being dreams that were kept at bay while the challenges of career, home-building and child-rearing were so absorbing. They might start a new business venture they have always fancied, like opening a country guest house. They may work at creating a rock garden, or take a trip around the world, or take an interest in helping a new theatre company. Or they may develop personal interests or skills they put aside earlier for lack of time—sculpture, or playing a musical instrument, or rebuilding vintage cars. They may decide to concentrate on improving their sex life, emphasising quality rather than quantity.

Whatever they do, they have the opportunity now to develop interests which serve as strands to link together their experiences up to now with their lifestyle in the later years.

Work, family and leisure come together

We see the operation of the 'triple helix' model in this little renaissance period. Dual-worker couples may have reached a position of achievement at work where they can use their work skills in an activity useful for leisure—the architect who becomes active in voluntary schemes for the rehabilitation of urban areas offers one example. Parents may put their family and child-rearing experiences to work in voluntary activities such as helping handicapped children.

Those who did not marry, or whose marriage broke up, leaving them single parents, may find companionship, with a neighbour, or a close friend from work or from a voluntary association, and build up a new domestic relationship on the basis of shared interests.

Work, family and leisure 'careers' interact and combine with

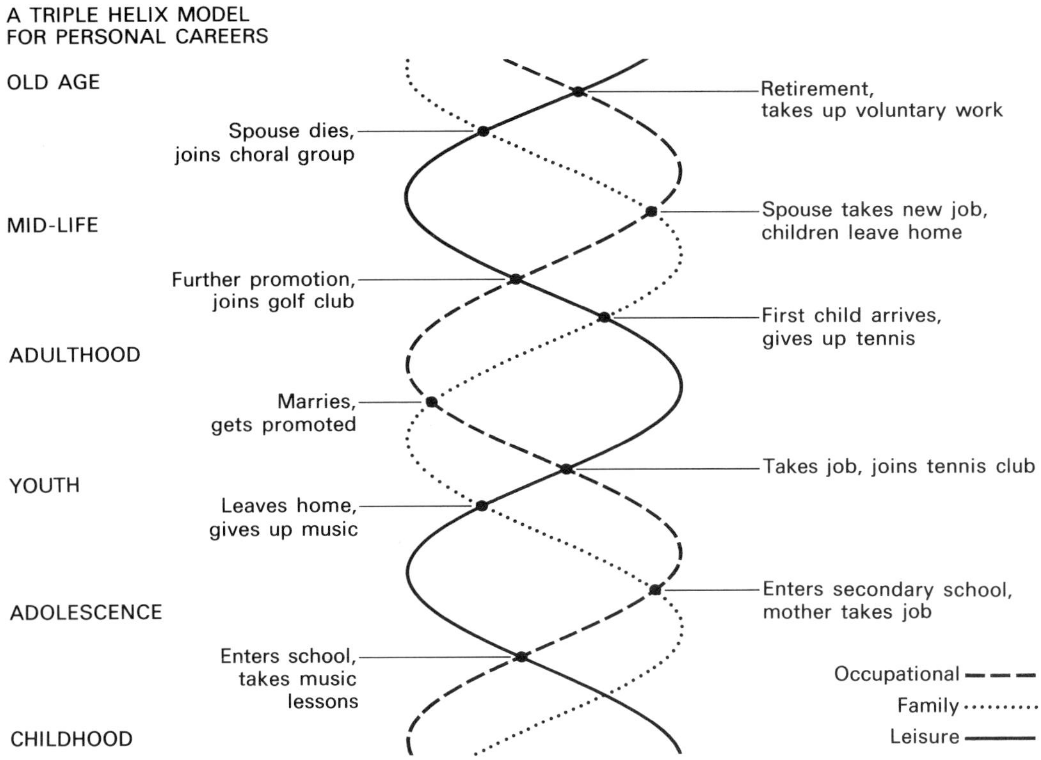

each other. As children grow up, they may be able to join more in the interests of their parents (boating, cooking, music, travel) and become more like friends than like children in the earlier sense. Or they may embark on the same or a related occupation, becoming their parents' colleagues.

As parents slacken off in their career commitments, their children may spark off in them an interest which they then pursue in their spare time. A journalist, for example, may take an interest in his son's work in marine archaeology and drop his press job to write books on the underwater world, or go on an expedition to the China Seas. A teacher may decide to leave the school where she has worked for thirty years and try self-sufficiency in the country where her children have lived in a commune. A political leader or industrial manager may decide to leave his job before retirement age to take up a charitable role in an organisation helping children with problems like those his own suffered.

But there are many—and no one knows how large this submerged passive subgroup is—who have no exciting, revitalising interests. Their acceptance of ageing is acquiescent. They feel finished, that they are old and life has passed them by, and they settle into a vegetative existence—set in their habits, in a rut at work, sitting at home watching television, unstimulated and unstimulating. They have, quite literally, lost interest in life. Their growth potential to meet the challenges of the phase to come is very low indeed.

6 Lifestyles for later years

We live in a society which measures much of the value of its adult members by their production *(in which we include, as we said in the last chapter,* reproduction*). Or to put it another way, people's self-esteem depends a good deal on feeling that they are fulfilling an occupational role, or a parental role (or both). This emphasis on the value of production is one reason why most people dread old age, and why so many feel bereaved when they retire, or when their youngest children finally leave home and they suffer from the empty nest feeling of no longer having the daily experience of parenthood.*

Fewer men are working after the legal age of retirement. Employment is also declining below the statutory age of retirement, because of earlier retirement, redundancy, increased unemployment, and what is classified as 'long-term sickness' (which may be a face-saving device used by the redundant—it is less of a stigma to register as sick than to be unemployed). These trends are present not only in Britain, but in other countries, notably the USA and Scandinavia, so the shift from paid employment to a productive life after retirement is assuming greater urgency.[1]

A painful passage

The transition from being a fully employed member of the community to being retired can be one of the most painful passages with which we are concerned in this book. But, as we have constantly stressed, life comprises not only paid work (or active parenthood), but also a network of social relationships, personal interests and associations, including some which have been dormant since youth because of lack of time.

A sense of relief

For many people their work has *not* been the most important or satisfying part of their lives; it may even have been a negative experience, and more enthusiasm may have been put into other things. The same, of course, may be true of parenthood and family life. If the task of coping with adolescents has been

Finding satisfaction in 'unproductive' activities—the challenge in later years.

exhausting and heightened marital discord, the departure of the children may be a relief. There are many indications in new research that the later years have unrecognised potential for *enjoyment*. At occupational retirement, those who have been lucky enough to love their life's work may have the opportunity to find a part-time or unpaid version of it. Those who have disliked the work that earned them their living will have the relief of giving it up. In either case there will be more time for learning to enjoy other, non-work, interests.

The long wait

But it is tragic and unnecessary that unknown numbers of otherwise healthy elderly people simply let themselves slip into premature old age and wait passively for death. We believe that this is partly because they have not had the opportunities to cultivate interests which would keep them stimulated all through life: they have had too little chance for education, too much pressure to throw themselves into work, or, in the case of women, too much isolation as 'captive wives' with no hope of getting their children looked after by someone else occasionally. We believe that our society as a whole could play a much more active part both in stimulating people's interests, and in making it physically possible for them to pursue them (by providing an adult education institute, a swimming pool, a village hall, or a cheaper and more reliable transport system). But the problems of passivity and distress observed among the elderly cannot be entirely laid at the door of the social system and its deficiences. To some extent it is due to lack of confidence and looking too much to others for solutions.

Harmony with the world

Taking it easy.

The main preoccupation of the later years is achieving a sense of *social and personal integration*, a sense of harmony with the world, and reconciliation with one's own life taken as a whole. It is also the time when people learn to live with the idea of dying. We believe that, although there is an overlap from the late establishment phase, this preoccupation with integration comes to the fore for most people in their late fifties. The major landmark is likely to be occupational retirement, usually at the statutory age of 60 or 65.

In traditional societies the old have more favourable conditions for achieving this sense of social and personal integration. In such societies, except in conditions of extreme hardship where physical stamina is at a premium, the elders of the tribe are revered and valued for the contributions they can make *because* of their age. They have accumulated knowledge, wisdom, experience and a sense of perspective. And the knowledge and skills they have acquired since youth do not become out of date with each passing year.

In contrast, ageing in our society seems the equivalent of obsolescence. As sociologist Irving Rosow has pointed out we have no adequate roles for older people, with the consequence that we systematically deprive them.[2] That is one of the reasons we avoid thinking about it in advance—a fact reflected in the way so many of us neglect to make adequate funeral or even pension arrangements. We feel, 'It won't happen to me.' But it almost certainly will. Men who have reached the age of 60 have an average life expectancy of 15·5 years, and women of 20·2 years. And that is allowing for all deaths, including accidents, before three score years and ten. So though some people die in their sixties or earlier, many survive into their eighties and even their nineties. That means that, demographically, old people are an increasingly important section of the population. In the United Kingdom, for example, the proportion aged over 65 rose from 5·4 per cent in 1911 to 13·2 per cent in 1971; and of persons over 60, from 7·9 per cent to 18·7 per cent. This change in the age structure of the population is a world-wide phenomenon, and is associated with the extension of people's life expectations.[3] From an average life-expectancy of about 30 years in pre-modern societies, individuals born in modern societies can expect, on average, to live until their late 70s.

So it is more important than ever to come to grips with the issues which can make old age a satisfying experience. Most people growing up now will have parents, grandparents and other relatives in this age group for a considerable proportion of their lives. Most will spend one third of their own lives in the over-60 age group, and move increasingly into grandparental and great-grandparental roles. Ethel Shanas calls these people the 'new pioneers', as half of all people aged over 65 will have families that span four generations, with many new challenges in what is largely uncharted social territory.[4]

The genuine age

Far from the madding crowd.

One of the blessings of old age is that one may develop a life style which is genuinely one's own—not status-seeking, not competitive, not calculating, not geared to future benefits, but devoted to present pleasures and the enjoyment of today. One is free, at last, to do what one wants (so long as one knows what that is).

A number of social theorists have pointed out that in a society as well-off as ours, old people should feel that they have a right to indulge themselves after a lifetime of hard work. Their retirement has been earned, it is not a 'gift' from the rest of us, nor should it be seen as a burden on those who are now producing. In fact older people, by indulging themselves, may well be able to contribute to society by showing the rest of us how to live—and by growing old gracefully (or even riotously) lift from their juniors their fear of the future.

Active until 80

Fortunately, contrary to popular belief, old age does not necessarily mean ill health. Certainly, many elderly people are plagued by chronic ailments such as arthritis, rheumatism, and cardiovascular or respiratory conditions. But relatively few people who have access to modern medicine are completely disabled before their late seventies. Researchers in the United States have found that most elderly people remain active despite their ailments until they are in their late seventies. So they should not be prematurely put on the shelf.

Retirement: common fears

What do people dread most about retirement? For men it appears to be the drop in their income, for women the loss of the companionship of their colleagues and workmates. Some research has shown that fears about health and one's ability to manage financially are most acute just *before* retirement rather than after. There is a kind of panic in anticipation of the passage out of the world of work. According to how these fears are coped with, adjustment to retirement will be easy or difficult. Yet there is a reluctance to come to terms with the issues in late middle age: employers do not wish their employees to turn their minds too much to these matters too soon, and the older workers themselves prefer to act as though nothing is going to happen. Nevertheless, we believe that people could be greatly helped in this transition period by being prepared for it, with appropriate help from such organisations as the Pre-Retirement Association.

Once the step to retirement has been made, side-benefits emerge—such as spending more time with one's children.

More men than women are willing to retire at the statutory age. There are a number of reasons for this. The statutory retirement age for women is earlier than for men. Many women's jobs tend to be less arduous, and many married women have to a certain extent taken outside employment as a voluntary activity—they are doing what they have chosen to do. Often they have taken up work later in life, having waited for the children to grow up. They have taken to it with a stored up energy and enthusiasm and do not wish to give it up so soon after. Single women are keener to retire than married women; perhaps because many married women will only have been working for ten or 15 years and will not be suffering yet from career fatigue. In this sense, single women resemble men; but they have the additional advantage of not having a partner to support, and may feel that the lower pension available at earlier retirement will be adequate.

How the retired fare

What do people actually do after retirement? Here there is rather more information. Some people simply continue pursuing the activities they enjoyed before retirement. Fishing (particularly for men), gardening and sexual activity (which, contrary to another cultural myth, may remain a source of pleasure for older people) are examples. And where people had few interests before

Interests enjoyed before retirement can be indulged more fully in later years.

retirement, they have little to build on following the event. In general, old people are more likely than younger ones to engage in less physically active pursuits—watching TV, reading, sitting, walking or just thinking. The better-off go sight-seeing or for drives. (Idleness as a way of passing the time—looking out of the window, napping, just sitting—is more characteristic of the very old.)

Research shows that the level of education, income and health has a significant influence. Where the level of all three is high, then an old person is likely to be relatively active—and find his or her activities satisfying. (We don't only mean physical activity. This would include meditation, reminiscence, conversation.) Where even *one* of the three is low, he or she is more likely to be passive—and unsatisfied. It does not seem surprising that poor health should affect one's satisfaction, but one's level of education is just as crucial, which confirms the great importance of this factor in preparing us to discover and develop our interests. In a unique study of women's post-retirement adjustment, Ruth Jewson found that women's patterns, whether professional or non-professional, differed from men's in the degree to which they sustained *social* involvements, with kin, former colleagues and voluntary associations.[5]

Is it too late to learn? Researchers in France, Britain and the USA have noted that the capacity to learn is affected by previous educational experience: those who learned well in youth, and have had further periods of learning, find it much easier to learn in later life. Unfortunately, our educational system is not yet geared to teaching people to learn throughout life, which is unfortunate, because the speed of technological change means that people now have to be ready to learn new things throughout life (from driving a car to using a calculating machine). Our present population of old people mostly left school at the age of 13 or 14; the generation behind them, now in the establishment phase, stayed on at school until 15 or 16—and a far higher proportion of them went on to further education. They may well prove better able to cope with old age than those we have data on at present.

Working beyond retirement

For a variety of reasons, many people wish to work beyond retirement age. For many the financial plight is acute—and made worse in Britain by compulsory retirement and the 'earnings rule' which confiscates part of their old age pension if they go on working and earn more than a very small weekly income. Those with private means or good occupational pensions can better afford to retire, and if they are not part of a large organisation, they may also have an occupation which they can continue part-time well beyond retirement, such as practising a profession, writing, sitting on boards or committees or holding consultancies. Often they continue part-time and gradually tail off as strength and inclination decline. At the lower end of the scale, certain occupations are open to older people—commissionaire, warden, custodian, chauffeur—but probably not nearly enough. Able-bodied older people with few qualifications continue to do odd jobs on a self-employed basis and at their own pace. A recent OECD report has urged that retirement schemes should be much more flexible to allow for such options.

In traditional societies, retirement from productive work allows more time for another kind of work in the upbringing of the new generations.

We believe that flexibility will be of particular benefit to women, who, as we have seen, are more reluctant to retire than men. Yet at present women are obliged to retire five years earlier from many occupations—with a lower pension. This is not only unjust, because earlier retirement puts a brake on the promotion prospects of career women, it is also anomalous because women live longer than men. Women of 65 or 70 are likely to be in better health than men of the same age. This may reflect their more sheltered role, as much as any biological resistance to the killing diseases of old age, but at present they are not given any options to test themselves through formal work.

Because of our fear of old age, there is considerable prejudice against older people in workplaces, ostensibly on the grounds that they have less strength or agility and a poorer memory. They are sometimes held to be difficult to get along with and crotchety, particularly older women. (Since most selection of candidates is done by men, this may reflect sexist prejudices. Women often feel desperately conscious, not just for 'sexual' reasons, of the need to look younger than their real age in order to cope with these prejudices.) In fact social-psychological research has confirmed that older people have specific strengths—reliability, judgement and loyalty.

To continue working, or to work part-time, should ideally be options open to people throughout their sixties. But they should not have to work, for financial reasons, if they would prefer to retire. Better pensions and no restrictions about drawing them would mean that older people could exercise a genuine choice between working and not working. Again, many people want to continue working, even at something they do not particularly like, because they cannot bear the thought of empty days; an approach to education which encourages the development of interests, and a community in which pursuing interests is made easier for everyone, even those with low levels of resourcefulness, is desirable. 'Not working' can increasingly be seen as providing an opportunity to do something more interesting or more enjoyable.

Grandparenting

Recent research has indicated that elderly people are generally less isolated from their families than has been feared and assumed. Censuses show that a fairly small proportion of households contain an elderly relative, but social surveys indicate that older people live close to their children's families and visit regularly. Some people deplore the lack of a granny in the family household, as in days of yore and emphasise not only the benefits of child care, but the specially friendly relations that can develop between members of alternating generations. Others feel there is no place for grandparents in the modern independent household, psychologically or physically: a two- or three-bedroomed family semi has no spare room. But one seldom-appreciated reason for some of the apparent isolation is that granny actually wants to live on her own, and in her own home, as long as possible.

We now know that there are more contacts between the generations than sociologists previously thought. The children of the elderly tend to live near their parent or parents, they visit them frequently, and they offer them a good deal of support. This seems to be the way both sides prefer it, as long as the elderly person's health holds out. Even in the United States, where so many people move long distances when they are promoted or change jobs, 80 per cent of older people live within an hour's drive of at least one of their children. In Great Britain and Denmark the proportion is nearly 90 per cent. The likelihood of living nearby is greater in solid working class communities and in agricultural communities than among individuals from white-collar and professional backgrounds, who are usually more mobile but also have more money to take trips home.

Another way to earn a crust!

The have-nots

Labour-saving devices enable most old people to manage on their own much longer than they might have done, and the telephone keeps them in touch with the younger generation. But one third of all old people in the US are classified 'deprived and frustrated' living below the poverty line without phones or other luxuries. Children vary in their willingness to stay in touch, not only with parents with whom they experienced difficulties but also with parents with whom they had 'good' relationships. There are some old people who have no contact of any kind with their families—not with their children, or with their brothers and sisters. And of course there are others who do not have any children or other relatives. They are a group particularly in need of help and concern.

Close but not too close

Most elderly people, though, enjoy being 'close but not too close' to their children and grandchildren, even their great-grandchildren. There is the opportunity, and the challenge, of sustaining diplomatic and mutually constructive relationships with offspring. The key, once again, lies in a lively, but not too heavy, sharing of interests. Sociologists and psychologists find that older people themselves prefer a combination of *distance* and *involvement*, what an Austrian expert on old age has called 'revocable detachment'.[6]

A flexible role

A number of recent studies indicate that a number of factors affect the styles with which people approach grandparenting—their personalities, the relationships they previously had with their children, their location and their values and resources. The role is vaguely defined, highly flexible and somewhat idealised. One researcher has described a situation in which granny was defined as a specially reliable and beloved baby-sitter. As early as 1953, sociologist Marvin Sussman described how grandparents were often used as 'house-sitters'.[7] He also traced the financial exchanges between generations—a two-way transaction, according to circumstances. Assessments of how happy older people are with these various arrangements have varied. Helena Lopata, in her study of widows in the Chicago area, recorded their disgruntlement in exquisite detail;[8] Bernice Neugarten and her colleagues, taking a more optimistic, growth-oriented approach, emphasised the potential for satisfaction in this role[9].

Whatever the pattern, it is clear that grandparenting, and indeed great-grandparenting, is a role that requires growth if one is to derive as much satisfaction as possible from it.

In-laws: a case for caution

Those who are in contact have relationships which, naturally, vary from close—constantly in each other's pockets—to cool or quarrelsome. They need to cultivate diplomacy, for this is a classically awkward relationship, unlike grandparenting. Elderly parents are fearful of hearing a son-in-law or daughter-in-law ask 'Do we *have* to go to your mother's again?' Relationships may have to be revised, especially when the parent is widowed. Sometimes an elderly woman will gladly help her working daughter or daughter-in-law. Sometimes, if she is working herself, or dislikes accepting her daughter's instructions, however graciously put, she will not. Needless to say, it requires a great deal of tact and maturity to strike the right note. But readiness to withdraw from closeness when tension is in the air, and the acceptance of that withdrawal without hurt feelings, may prevent disagreements, which are natural between two adult generations, from exploding into quarrels.

We distinguish three sub-phases in later years, each with its own preoccupation.

The run-in to retirement

In the five years or so before retirement, the main preoccupation of most people is *anticipation.* That includes pretending it is not going to happen, trying to make it happen as soon as possible in order to get it over with, as well as looking forward to the good things retirement will bring and making sensible plans for the future.

Making the crossing from working to retirement can be a hazardous one—or another period of growth.

The middle-aged are conscious that they are moving towards a state of life which is not much valued in our society. Mostly they do not want to be old; they may avoid older people and pretend that they themselves are not as old as they are, and even avoid their own age group.

The balance between husband and wife may change. Ten years ago he may have been at the peak of his career and she may have been suffering from the empty nest syndrome and loss of self-esteem; now she may have regained her confidence through some outside occupation, while he feels he is about to be overtaken by younger men. Later, when he retires, there may be difficulty if her income is greater than his pension. Or if she has filled her life with home-making and nothing else they may no longer have much in common, and their relationship may have become what some American studies have called the 'hollow-shell marriage', in which the partners stay together only because each feels it is too late to make another start. A number of researchers have noted in both sexes the reawakening of a sense of closeness to brothers, sisters and other relatives, as well as the reawakening of religious interests.

Facing the void

Retirement is often an unthinkable event, particularly for men, since Western society has put a high value for men on being 'gainfully employed'. Work structures most of their waking lives, sets the pattern of their relationships, and occupies their thoughts. Work makes them 'real' men, good providers, and even 'good' people. The idea of living without working may arouse images of a meaningless, frightening, undefined void, and considerable anxiety, especially just before retirement. For single people, both men and women, retirement may also mean the loss of perhaps their most important human relationships. All these things inhibit people from making adequate preparation for retirement.

Good employers now know that the presentation of a gold watch is not an adequate way to help their staff face retirement, if interesting as a *rite de passage*. It has become an important part of personnel work to prepare employees for retirement and help them plan their future. Trade unions have traditionally regarded retirement reforms as one of their main concerns, and pensions are a major plank of political election programmes.

Quite apart from retirement itself, many people will face a complete change of lifestyle, moving house, for instance, and perhaps fixing up another occupation. There is no doubt that, psychologically, the best way to *cope* with this transition is to *face* it—and here, outside advice can be a great support. There may have to be financial and legal rearrangements—property to transfer, annuities to buy, wills to make. These tasks will not just go away if the individual refuses to recognise that old age is near, or refuses to countenance change.

However, people vary greatly in the resourcefulness with which they rearrange their lives at this crucial moment, and consequently in the amount of outside assistance they need. But we believe strongly that assistance should be available if wanted—and particularly for those who are showing least initiative. For them above all it might make an immense difference to the 20 years ahead of them.

It's never too late to learn

The idea of retirement as another life-career stage may help people who have been deeply committed to one particular adult work role to accept that they can have, and enjoy, other occupations. For this, seeing education as a life-long process is important. Retraining courses, the Open University in Britain, adult education and other parts of our formal educational system are starting to meet these needs, but there are numerous barriers and constraints, even beyond the formidable financial ones.

One of them is the fact that retirement has so often tended to be seen as a time of pure 'leisure'. This notion may inhibit people from taking an active part in redeploying their interests and involvements in ways suitable for later life. It also implies that people at this stage do not need to, or are not capable of, new learning. But research in France and Britain, as well as in the USA, has shown that work-training undertaken at a much later age than traditionally (age 41–55) is far more effective than anyone expected, and there is 'near-parity between younger and older learners'. This kind of training could be extended to 'teach' older people to develop their interests. Well educated people, as we have indicated, are often resourceful in creating their own new learning situations, but they can benefit from such schemes as much as poorly educated people, even if the latter appear to have more need of them. For although well educated people have a wider range of interests with which to face retirement, if their work has been stimulating those interests may have taken the form of relatively passive and restful activities (like reading or listening to music); and they may need prodding into more energetic pursuits to compensate for the loss of demanding work.

The experience of life that older people bring to new learning can sometimes give them an edge over younger ones.

Once retirement arrives . . .

Once they have retired, older people's main preoccupation is *realignment*—reorganising their lives and getting used to all the changes—which may involve living in a new place as well as embarking on a new occupation. At first, retirement may feel like a holiday, bringing with it a sense of relief or euphoria, a 'honeymoon' quality—but as with younger unemployed people (discussed in Chapter 4) that feeling may soon be followed by depression and apathy.

Fewer roles to play

This is a time of what sociologists call 'multiple role loss'. Quite apart from the loss of a lifetime's occupation, there tends to be a loss of relationships associated with the job—clients, customers, colleagues, and the round of people one encounters in the course of work. There may be a severe loss of self-esteem, even for those who have soon lined up another occupation for themselves. Unless one is fortunate, or at the other extreme if one's health and abilities are very poor, one is likely to gravitate towards jobs that are less demanding—and therefore lower paid and of lower status. It may come as a shock to learn that people regard one as an 'old man', lucky to get any kind of work. This is less of a problem for, say, a street-cleaner who redeploys himself as a caretaker, a maintenance man or a groundsman; but for a manager to find himself given such tasks would require psychological adjustments of a fairly radical kind. On the other hand, professional and managerial workers are better off financially and may have the kind of contacts to find themselves new occupations that more nearly coincide with their view of themselves. Many of them work part-time at quasi-managerial or consultancy jobs, perhaps with honorific titles to compensate for low pay.

Loss of work status has in the past been more painful for a man than a woman because public opinion still does not expect a woman's work to be part of her identity (though it may be painful for the manager's wife). But the contrast is likely to diminish as women's identities come to be more closely connected with their jobs or careers.

Sex and class make a difference

Retirement has a different significance for husbands and wives in conventional families. A British study of older couples in Bristol found that 35 per cent of wives look forward to seeing more of their husbands when they retire; but only 15 per cent of the husbands look forward to seeing more of their wives.[10] In practice, things may turn out unexpectedly; many conventional men do not understand that their wives' lives are organised around the central fact that they are not there during the day; and many women find it tiresome to have their husbands under their feet all day, however much they thought, in advance, they would like it. 'I married him for better or worse, but not for lunch' is a classic retirement joke.

There are class differences too. Manual workers fear retirement less than non-manual—perhaps because they are giving up less, both in satisfaction and in salary—but they find it more difficult

In some societies there's no such thing as 'retirement'—just a change of emphasis.

to adjust to a home and family-centred lifestyle, and they are less resourceful, having generally lower levels of education, in developing new interests. Middle class men are better at the task of 'realignment', because they are more accustomed to learning. Their stock in trade has been what psychologist Donald Michael has called 'learning to plan—and planning to learn', and are in any case more family-centred; but they find the loss of status harder to bear.[11] Both American and British studies have shown that it is primarily a tendency of middle class people to deny that they are growing old, and to dissociate themselves as long as possible from identifying with their age group.

How much activity?

Professional opinions vary as to how the adjustment to retirement is best made. Social psychologist Robert Havighurst has demonstrated that the development of variegated interests at earlier stages is helpful, but not automatically.[12] A certain degree of continuity is desirable, but also necessary is a degree of change and realignment of interests. Solitary hobbies, for example, might have been soothing at the peak of a hectic work life, but after retirement they may add to the feeling of loneliness. People have to give up physically demanding activities as their health and strength declines. Family leisure activities will probably become more intermittent. In the early years after retirement, Havighurst has shown, the tendency is to re-assess and restructure one's activities, using the fact that one has free time, while others are working, to get out and about—travelling, visiting and so on. Later, one becomes more housebound.

One theory, popular early in the century, was that people should keep *engaged* as long as possible. But more recently, psychologist William Henry and sociologist Elaine Cumming have proposed the theory of *disengagement*.[13] They found that retired people tend to *want* to withdraw, not only from activities but from social relationships too, and they concluded that the need to withdraw is adaptive for older people. In their view withdrawal is actually healthier both for the individual and for the community, because it prepares the ageing for the approach of death and lessens the otherwise traumatic effect their decline would have on themselves and their death would have on the social system.

The pros and cons of 'engagement'

There is, of course, value in both these views. 'Engagement', particularly as it refers to continued work, gives continued meaning to an old person's life and structures their time. On the other hand, it may, by apparently endorsing the whole complex of work and activity as life's most worthwhile pursuits, prevent old people from putting a higher value on enjoyment—which it is widely felt should be the keynote of later years. However, we must remember that the later years stage may nowadays last for decades, not a few years, and while withdrawal as early as 60 or 65 is not usually a satisfying response to retirement, it may be felt to be desirable 15 or 20 years later, or when illness and handicap finally make themselves felt.

Not enough is known about the psychology of growth in old age. Much more is known about older people as a 'population at risk'—from apathy, depression, suicide, loneliness and so on—than about their potential for happiness. But we know from studies of the family cycle that, although happiness and satisfaction tend to decline from a pinnacle during early married life, there can be an up-turn in late life, when couples make a new relationship once their children have left home and formal careers are over.

Ways to meet the challenge

There seem to be three ways in which people can meet the challenge of retirement in a positive way.

The psychological approach: cultivating joy

The first is to cultivate a capacity for joy. This is a capacity for which one's experience as an infant is crucial. The way feelings of love and hate, anger and envy, optimism and despair are handled early in life is the foundation for happiness all through life; and happiness in later life depends on achieving a better understanding of one's inner motivations, inhibitions and strengths. But learning and growth can occur throughout life, and with it, the capacity for joy. Even old age is not too late for learning to come to terms with oneself. Sometimes expert help is useful, but resources being limited, this is not available for everyone; the surest resource is oneself and one's immediate environment—partner, relations and, above all in old age, friends.

The activity approach: a middle option

A second approach (put here by Englishman Beric Wright) is more organisational than psychological, but of course has important psychological benefits:

> The man who dies of a broken heart soon after retirement is a classic case of too little challenge or stresslessness. He has his house, his pension and his family, but he has lost his identity, his purpose and his status. He has nothing to do and nowhere to go—so he fizzles gently out from emotional deprivation. Success in retirement depends on a lot of things, but one of the most important factors is happily to shed the anxieties, or boredom, pressure and routine of going to work every day and replacing them with purposeful enjoyable activity which keeps you gently on the hop until bedtime.[14]

This middle-range option is the one most readily available.

The social approach: communities for the old

There is a third, *social* approach, which has been deliberately tried, mostly in Canada and the USA. That is the creation of new communities expressly for old people.

There have been many differences of professional opinion about the merits of 'mixed' vs 'homogeneous' living arrangements. But whatever the conclusion, there are clearly many older people who prefer one another's company. Many older Americans with enough money have clubbed together in 'Sun Cities', which have mushroomed in states with a favourable climate. There are 'fun-oriented' towns where no resident under 50 is allowed and where many of the citizens are, as they say, '80 years young'. In these Sun Cities—sometimes called 'Leisure Worlds' or 'Youngtowns'—cultural patterns are preserved like flies in amber, according to the tastes of the age groups that inhabit them; and the inhabitants are able to live happily together without fear of mugging, riots, hippies, smog, campus unrest or inter-racial tensions. Here no one disparages people for being old; no one has to 'keep up' with competitive performance norms, and cultural and technological change are kept at bay. There are few new fads and fashions—but time for reminiscences, favourite films, old-style dancing, pottery classes, keep-fit and so on.

In Canada, too, there are retirement villages which cater for the tastes of older people and, above all, provide friendly communities. The Canadians are, like the Americans, discussing the possibility of communal living groups for the elderly—an idea which is already a reality in Sweden.

There are no 'affluent ghettoes' of quite this type in Britain, although there are some purpose-built housing developments for the elderly and some places (Bournemouth, Eastbourne) are heavily populated with old people who are fulfilling their dream of living by the sea—a recurrent longing of the British. Better-off British people may retire even further south—to Mallorca or the Costa del Sol in Spain; but the reality is often different from the dream, as living there all the year round is not a permanent summer holiday, and some regret being so far away from their family and old friends.

Having fun and facing fears

All the same, people do take on a 'new lease of life' in these elderly communities, which appear to be exceptionally successful in enabling their inhabitants to enjoy themselves—in spite of, in many cases, the inhibiting effects of a puritan upbringing imbued with the work ethic. Living like this also seems to overcome some of the terrors of facing eventual disablement and death, by bringing people's natural fears into the open.

The main anxieties of this period are about becoming ill, and being far from one's family when one may need help, particularly as one moves into the late seventies. There may be a very strong feeling of *not* wanting to be a burden, the more so if one has lost one's partner. There are also likely to be practical problems about money, housing and social relationships. Communities for the elderly address themselves to all these areas, thereby relieving psychological as well as practical burdens. For there are no terrors so great as those which remain unconscious—especially about something as basic as who will care for one in old age, and perhaps shed a tear at one's grave.

Old age

Old people and young people do not always find it easy to tolerate one another gladly.

With better health and a different attitude to life, people are active longer—and with luck they do not enter the stage of 'old age' until they are in their mid-seventies. This is the period at which their main preoccupation is with *life before death.*

By now, people are quite likely to have lost their husbands or wives and many of the friends and relatives of their own generation. If younger relatives have moved away, as often happens, the old people will be more isolated than they were at 60. Taking grandchildren—or even great-grandchildren—on outings or giving them treats becomes more difficult, both physically and financially. Much of the pleasure may go out of it, particularly if one feels that one is a burden or a bore. Old people become prey to increasing loneliness and insecurity about feeling unwanted. A growing proportion of old people remarry—but there are problems involved. Neither partner finds it easy to change habits or to develop tolerance.

This is an age of special vulnerability to physical disorders, and to the psychological distress that comes with ageing. Illnesses like arteriosclerosis, uraemia, diabetes and strokes are more likely, and so are accidents and injuries from falls. Poorer people may suffer from malnutrition and from hypothermia in winter. And 'behaviour' problems in old age are part and parcel of the physical problems. Untidiness, forgetfulness, repeating oneself, childishness all increase the old person's suffering, if he or she is conscious of them, and may make helping more difficult.

Prescriptions for fulfilment: community . . .

Most advanced countries recognise their responsibilities to senior citizens, however imperfectly they fulfil them. There are many specialist organisations which concern themselves with old people's problems, and there is provision either for supervising or for rehousing them when they get too old to look after themselves and there is no relative to live with. There is some controversy both among professionals and in families where the decisions have to be taken about what forms this help should take. But old people themselves mostly dislike institutions such as old people's homes, where they are segregated from the community and live in a world of rules and regulations; they prefer the semi-segregated type of housing where flatlets or bungalows are grouped together, perhaps in the care of a warden, perhaps with communal club rooms or dining rooms, where they can live as independently as they wish and are able. (Other people cling to their independence to the last, and are often found living in squalor, half-starved. Some will require hospital care.)

Old people are prone to compare their present selves with themselves in the past—and feel depressed in consequence; one sociologist has termed this state of mind 'desolation'. The great virtue of semi-segregated housing or elderly resorts is that the old people who live there can compare themselves not with their previous selves but with all their contemporaries who live there, which is psychologically a less depressing comparison. There are always others more feeble, more wrinkled, more forgetful. There is another advantage: because they are no longer part of the workaday world they can make their own timetables to suit themselves and as a consequence feel less out of step. And they are 'all in the same boat'—fewer relatives, similar problems and anxieties—so they can support and comfort each other.

. . . interests . . .

People over 75 are in general less able to be physically active, but they may still be very lively mentally, even if their eyesight or hearing is less than it was. And they can continue to learn. The importance of supplying the means whereby they can continue to develop and pursue meaningful interests cannot be too much emphasised—whether it is to make sure that spectacles are adequate for reading, or supplying a wheelchair so that the old person can get to a library to choose books or records. Keeping up appearances, whether having one's hair styled or buying a new hat, is also immensely important for morale. A telephone may, at this stage, be a vital lifeline with the outside world as well as a way of staying in touch with friends and relatives. Pets are also found to be useful in helping older people to feel needed—even if only to feed the budgerigar—and for company. All these things keep depression and senility at bay.

. . . and religion

Interest in religion may grow at this age; traditionally it helps the old face death with peace in mind. Recently, with religious belief less part of the lives of people, there have been efforts to provide secular substitutes for the consolations of religion. In psychiatry, for example, there is now much interest in the phenomenology of dying—helping dying people and those close to them to face death.

In their final years, old people cling to things they know, their treasured objects, their home, people and memories. They remember the distant past more clearly than yesterday. At this stage of life, losses are suffered as 'psychic wounds', and for the elderly person the work of bereavement is particularly painful. In early retirement it is 'dysfunctional' (harmful to development) to try to keep lost relationships alive: thus the widow who always feels her lost husband is 'with her', shuts off the possibility of making other relationships. In these last months or years, on the other hand, this living in the past—or pretending that the past is still alive—brings about a sense of the wholeness and completion of life. At this final stage, when one is mentally integrating one's whole life, 'disengagement' makes sense.

7 The whole life

All that we have been discussing in this book makes nonsense, we believe, of the commonly held notion that emotional maturity and the capacity to adapt to and enjoy the challenge of adult life are necessarily determined once-and-for-all by a set of experiences in early childhood. This is not to deny that such experiences do sometimes have an overwhelming effect.

We do not believe that the adult is necessarily *'set for life' by late adolescence, when biological growth stops. In fact, we feel strongly that the biological model is not adequate when considering the development of the whole person. Nor is the psychoanalytical model—which is too much based on clinical experience with individuals who have* failed *to cope with the challenges of life. Clinicians rarely see the many people who have responded well to those challenges despite a poor start in life.*

A message of hope

We are optimistic about human potential. Every one of the major 'passages' of life, with its new set of challenges, offers new opportunities for growth. People have chances to grow all through life and eventually to arrive at old age with some feeling of psychological achievement and satisfaction—even if illness, disability or misfortune impose their own constraints. Certain elements are, however, essential.

Preoccupations

The preoccupations appropriate to one's stage in life have to be recognised, and ways found to deal with them. They cannot be ignored.

Interests

Interests are the means of giving form to preoccupations—so the cultivation of interests all through life is crucial to growth. It is through their interests that people develop their capacities and, often, form their most valuable relationships with others.

Resourcefulness

Resourcefulness is a necessary ingredient in acquiring and pursuing interests, and fitting them in with available channels for acting—for without activation an interest remains dormant, an unexpressed potential.

A sticky start can end up with a sweet finish.

The ingredients of growth

The veteran marriage counsellors David and Vera Mace have suggested three other essentials in their recent book *How to Have a Happy Marriage*: the ability and the desire to communicate; the ability to accept conflicts and to resolve them creatively; and commitment to growth—actually *wanting* to grow. Our own data and impressions also suggest that these are important ingredients in the personal growth process.

Helping the less fortunate

All these essentials are easier to write about than to put into practice, and some people have more success in achieving them than others. We believe that the fortunate among us have an immensely important part to play in assisting the less fortunate and the less resourceful. We can help them to find and pursue interests through which they, too, can find enjoyment and express their preoccupations satisfactorily. And when we are irritated by the fumbling of the old, or the self-absorption of the young, we would do well to remember that they may both, in their different ways, be trying to resolve the preoccupations of their particular stages of life.

Finding a larger awareness

It is often claimed that consciousness-raising inevitably leads to dissatisfaction. Awareness of the inequalities of class structures, sex roles, age differences and so on often has a disruptive effect. It becomes necessary to rethink and change the established patterns. This may be disturbing in the short run, when the complacency of the status quo is shattered, but in the long term it leads to fuller satisfaction. And in the long run it is the way to escape the despair that comes with passive acceptance of things that could, and should, change.

Each stage has its needs

Different stages of life have their own special needs. The mother who has spent years wrapped up in her children's development needs to redeploy her energies after they become independent. She feels something of a vacuum in her life if she has not prepared for this transition. Her problems will be different from those of a successful businessman at a similar age. He, too, may feel that his life lacks meaning. But in his case this may be not because he lacks interests, but because his involvements are out of key with his personal needs. Both need to confront themselves and their situations. Both need to clarify their values in order to make choices about the changes which are necessary and possible in their lives.

Self or society?

There are those who feel that it is self-indulgent to concentrate on personal fulfilment while there are larger social problems burning to be dealt with. Better to use one's energies to bring under control the social forces which block or constrain growth. But in our view it is not necessary to be in control of society, or even of one's own life, to be able to use one's energy productively. Take the case of a prisoner, John McGrath. Here we have an extreme example of someone not in control of his life and with the minimum of freedom of movement and interaction. Nevertheless, John McGrath studied through the Open University for a higher degree and on his release took up a university post in which his special experience was an advantage and his students benefited. Both kinds of effort are required.

Looking beyond the individual

It is important that we look to our own growth, but also beyond it, and do what we can to help society become a better place. This may or may not feed back directly into our own opportunity and reward system. But it is a necessity, simply because our society does not afford sufficient opportunity structures for interest development. And indeed many have found that a passion for social reform has provided a framework of interests which has given their own lives meaning.

Society itself has a vital part to play in helping all its citizens to enjoy life. In the formal social services priority is given to the vulnerable—the disabled, the disordered, the poor, the young, the old and the unemployed—but society is the rest of us too. There is an immense battle still to be waged to improve the quality of urban life. We must work towards better working conditions, education and provisions for leisure in order to enable everyone to pursue their interests.

We have tried in this book to indicate some of the ways in which people can foster their own growth. But this is not solely a matter for individuals. More of us can realise our growth potential if we live in a society that provides a conducive environment for us to do so. Society is people, and it is up to ordinary people to band together to make their needs and wants known and to make sure they are catered for.

References

1 The enterprise of living

1. Hall, G. Stanley. *Adolescence: Its Psychology and Its Relation to Physiology, Anthropology, Sociology, Sex, Crime, Religion and Education.* NY: Appleton, 1904.
2. Apostle, L., Mandelbrote, B. and Piaget, J. *Logique et équilibre.* Paris: Presses Universitaires de France, 1957.
3. See, for example, Levinson, D. *The Seasons of a Man's Life.* NY: Knopf, 1978.
4. Rapoport, R. Normal crises, family structure and mental health, *Family Process*, 1963, 68–80.
5. Hill, R. and Rodgers, R. H. The developmental approach 1. In Christensen, H. T. (ed.) *Handbook of Marriage and the Family.* Chicago: Rand-McNally, 1964.
6. Caplan, G. *Support Systems and Community Mental Health.* NY. Behavioural Publications, 1974.
7. White, R. W. *The Study of Lives.* NY: Atherton, 1959.
8. Clark, K. E. Vocational interest testing. In *International Encyclopaedia of the Social Sciences.* NY: Crowell Collier and Macmillan, 1968, 16, 345–349.
9. Sheehy, G. *Passages: Predictable Crises of Adult Life.* NY: Dutton, 1976.

2 Childhood: a time for play

1. Ariès, P. *Centuries of Childhood: A Social History of Family Life.* NY: Knopf, 1962.
2. Bruner, J., Jolly, A. and Sylva, K. (eds.) *Play: Its Role in Development and Evolution.* Harmondsworth: Penguin, 1976.
3. Huizinga, J. *Homo Ludens: A Study of the Play Element in Culture.* London: Routledge and Kegan Paul, 1949.
4. Jones, E. G. *Children Growing Up.* Harmondsworth: Penguin, 1973, 105–106.
5. Bernstein, B. *Class, Codes and Control.* London: Routledge and Kegan Paul, 1971.
6. Opie, I. and P. *The Lore and Language of Schoolchildren.* Oxford: Clarendon, 1959.
7. Himmelweit, H. et al. *Television and the Child.* London: Oxford University Press, 1958; also see Wartella, E. (ed.) *Children Communicating.* Beverly Hills and London: Sage, 1979; and Pierce, C. M. (ed.) *Television and Education.* Beverly Hills and London: Sage, 1978.

3 Adolescence and the discovery of self

1. Blos, P. *The Adolescent Passage,* NY: International University Press, 1978.
2. Erikson, E. H. *Identity, Youth and Crisis.* NY: Norton, 1968.
3. Lidz, T. *The Person.* NY: Basic Books, 1968.
4. Freud, A. Adolescence, in Freud, A. et al. (eds.) *Psychoanalytic Study of the Child.* 13, 255–278. NY: International Universities Press, 1958.
5. Chilman, C. *Adolescent Sexuality in a Changing American Society.* United States Department of Health, Education and Welfare, 1978.
6. See Bone, M. *Family Planning Services: Changes and Effects.* London: HMSO, 1975.
7. Marcuse, H. *Eros and Civilisation.* Boston: Beacon, 1955.

8. Miller, D. *Adolescence.* NY: Jason Aronson, 1974. Also see Kenniston, K. *Youth and Dissent.* NY: Harcourt, 1971.
9. Eisenstadt, S. N. *From Generation to Generation.* Chicago: Free Press, 1965.
10. Kovar, L. C. *Faces of the Adolescent Girl.* Englewood Cliffs: Prentice-Hall, 1968.
11. Young, M. and McGeeney, P. *Learning Begins at Home.* London: Routledge and Kegan Paul, 1968.
12. Illich, I. D. *Deschooling Society.* NY: Harper and Row, 1971.
13. Gabor, D. *The Mature Society.* London: Secker and Warburg, 1972.
14. Matza, D. Position and behaviour patterns of youth. In Farris, R. E. L. (ed.) *Handbook of Modern Sociology.* Chicago: Chicago University Press, 1964.
15. Mead, M. *From the South Seas: Studies of Adolescence and Sex in Primitive Societies.* NY: Morrow, 1939.

4 The decade of young adulthood

1. Leonard, D. *Sex and Generation.* London: Tavistock, 1980.
2. Marris, P. *The Experience of Higher Education.* London: Routledge and Kegan Paul, 1964.
3. Kahl, J. A. Educational and occupational aspirations of 'Comman man' boys, *Harvard Educational Review,* 1953, 23, 186–203.
4. Summerskill, J. Dropouts from college. In Sanford, N. (ed.) *The American College.* NY and London: Wiley, 1962, 627–657.
5. Snyder, B. *Hidden Curriculum.* Cambridge, Mass: M.I.T. Press, 1972.
6. Sinberg, D. The widening gap: attitudes of first-year students and staff towards chemistry, science, careers and commitment, *Science Studies,* 1971, 287–313.
7. Marsden, D. *Workless.* Harmondsworth: Penguin, 1975.
8. Davis, F. *On Youth Subcultures: The Hippie Variant.* California: McCalib-Seiler, 1973.
9. Mills, R. *Young Outsiders in London.* London: Routledge and Kegan Paul, 1973.
10. See Abrams, P. and McCulloch, A. *Communes, Sociology and Society.* Cambridge: Cambridge University Press, 1976.

5 Establishment

1. Pleck, J. and Sawyer, J. (eds.) *Men and Masculinity.* Englewood Cliffs: Prentice-Hall, 1974.
2. Gronseth, E. Work sharing. In Rapoport, R. and Rapoport, R. N. (eds.) *Working Couples.* London: Routledge and Kegan Paul, 1978.
3. Riesman, D. Introduction to Seeley, J. et al. *Crestwood Heights.* NY: Basic Books, 1956.
4. Friedan, B. *The Feminine Mystique.* NY and London: Penguin, 1963.
5. Gavron, H. *The Captive Wife.* London: Routledge and Kegan Paul, 1966.
6. Rapoport, R. and Rapoport R. N. *Dual Career Families Re–examined.* London: Martin Robertson; NY: Harper and Row, 1976.
7. Young, M. and Willmott, P. *The Symmetrical Family.* London: Routledge and Kegan Paul, 1973.
8. Brown, G. and Harris, T. *Social Origins of Depression.* London: Tavistock, 1978.
9. Bernard, J. *The Future of Marriage.* Baltimore: Penguin, 1972.
10. Hunt, A. *Survey of Woman's Employment.* London: HMSO, 1968.
11. Rossi, A. A good woman is hard to find, *Transaction,* 1964, 2, 120–123.
12. Jaques, E. Death and the midlife crisis, *International Journal of Psychoanalysis,* 1965, 46, 4, 203–214.
13. Levinson, D. *op. cit.* 1978.
14. Horner, M. *op. cit.* 1972.
15. Peter, L. J. and Hull, R. *Peter Principle: Why Things Always Go Wrong.* NY. Souvenir Press, 1971.

6 Lifestyles for later years

1. Shanas, E., Townsend, P., Wedderburn, D., Friis, H., Milhoj, P. and Stehouwer, J. *Old People in Three Industrial Societies.* NY: Atherton; London: Routledge and Kegan Paul, 1968.
2. Rosow, I. *Socialisation to Old Age.* Berkeley: University of California Press, 1975.
3. Hauser, P. Aging and worldwide population change. In Binstock, R. and Shanas, E. (eds.) *Handbook of Aging and the Social Sciences.* NY: Van Nostrand Reinhold, 1976.
4. Shanas, E. *Older People and Their Families: New Pioneers.* Burgess Award Lecture, National Council on Family Relations, 1979. (*Journal of Marriage and the Family,* forthcoming.)
5. Jewson, R. H. *After Retirement: An Exploratory Study of Professional Women.* Ph.D. Thesis, University of Minnesota, 1978.
6. Rosenmayr, L. *Family Relations of the Elderly.* 7th International Congress of Gerontology, Vienna, 1966. Also, see Riley, M. W. and Foner, A. *Aging and Society.* NY: Russell Sage, 1968; and Townsend, P. *The Family Life of Old People.* London: Routledge and Kegan Paul.
7. Sussman, M. The help pattern in the middle class family, *American Sociological Review,* 1953, 18, 22–28. Also, see Sussman, M. The Family Life of Old People. In Binstock, R. and Shanas, E. (eds.) *op. cit.* 1976.
8. Lopata, H. Z. *Widowhood in an American City.* Cambridge, Mass: Schenckmann, 1973.
9. Neugarten, B. and Weinstein, K. The changing American grandparent, *Marriage and Family Living,* 1964, 26, 199–204. Also, see Neugarten, B. and Hagestad, G. O. Age and the Life Course. In Binstock, R. and Shanas, E. (eds.) *op. cit.* 1976.
10. Crawford, M. H. Retirement and disengagement, *Human Relations,* 1971, 24, 3, 255–278.
11. Michael, D. *Learning to Plan and Planning to Learn.* San Francisco: Jossey-Bass, 1973.
12. Havighurst, R. Flexibility and the social roles of the retired, *American Journal of Sociology,* 1954, 29, 4.
13. Cumming, E. M. and Henry, W. *Growing Old.* NY: Basic Books, 1961.
14. Wright, H. B. Stress and retirement, *Retirement Choice,* 1972, October.

Acknowledgements

We wish to thank Susan Raven for the excellent job she did under pressure in creating the draft from which this book emerged. It is based on our *Leisure and the Family Life Cycle* (London/Boston, Routledge and Kegan Paul, 1975). For a fuller view, the reader is referred to this work, and also to our *Fathers, Mothers and Others* (London, Routledge, 1977) published in the USA as *Fathers, Mothers and Society* by Basic Books, and in Spring 1980 as a paperback by Vintage Books, Random House. We wish to thank our co-author in these works, Ziona Strelitz, for her creative participation; and Stephen Kew, also of the Institute of Family and Environmental Research, for his collaboration in the second of the two books. Neither of our colleagues is, of course, responsible for any shortcomings of the present work.

Index

Photo credits

Aliza Auerbach—33, 90; Bob Bray—18 (*bottom*), 21, 25; Ron Chapman—24, 29, 84; Gadi Dagon—37; John Garrett—5; Susan Griggs/A. Woolfit—68; Richard and Sally Greenhill—10, 77; Israel Museum—76 (*top*); Kristal—76 (*bottom*); Sheelah Latham—23; Judy and Kenny Lester—94; Lisa Mackson—41, 43, 51, 52, 54, 59, 97, 101, 104, 109; Rex Features—13, 16, 20, 34, 40, 44, 45 (*2*), 65, 69, 72, 82, 102, 103, 105, 106, 108, 112 (*left*), 119, (Chris Capstick) 116, (Champlong/Arepi) 80, (Globe Photos) 10, 73, (Norman Potter) 111, (Sipa Press) 8, 12, 36, 47, 48, 112 (*right*) (Nigel Snowdon) 18 (*top*), 19; Homer Sykes—61.

Illustrator: Oxford Illustrators Ltd—99.

Authors' photographs by Sharin Smelser.